MW00815483

A LITTLE BIT

OF

CRYSTALS

A LITTLE BIT

OF

CRYSTALS

AN INTRODUCTION TO CRYSTAL HEALING

CASSANDRA EASON

STERLING ETHOS
New York

STERLING ETHOS
New York

An Imprint of Sterling Publishing Co., Inc.
1166 Avenue of the Americas
New York, NY 10036

This publication is a component of
A Little Bit of Crystals Kit (ISBN 978-1-4549-3824-8) and is not to be sold separately.

Distributed in Canada by Sterling Publishing Co., Inc.
c/o Canadian Manda Group, 664 Annette Street
Toronto, Ontario M6S 2C8, Canada
Distributed in the United Kingdom by GMC Distribution Services
Castle Place, 166 High Street, Lewes, East Sussex BN7 1XU, England
Distributed in Australia by NewSouth Books
University of New South Wales, Sydney, NSW 2052, Australia

For information about custom editions, special sales, and premium
and corporate purchases, please contact Sterling Special Sales
at 800-805-5489 or specialsales@sterlingpublishing.com.

Manufactured in China

2 4 6 8 10 9 7 5 3 1

sterlingpublishing.com

Cover design by Elizabeth Mihaltse Lindy

Image Credits
Katja Gerasimova/Shutterstock.com
satit_srihin/Shutterstock.com (border)

CONTENTS

INTRODUCTION

Crystals are the most exciting, powerful psychic tools, for they act as transmitters and amplifiers of health, happiness, love, success, and prosperity, and they enhance the home and workplace with both energy and protection.

If you wonder why crystals contain so much power, you should know that the oldest object found on Earth was a tiny fragment of zircon discovered in Western Australia that is 4.404 billion years old. The great antiquity of every crystal as well as its formation by rushing water, volcanic fire, the earth, and the winds give crystals a depth that connects with our innate spiritual nature.

Crystals release this power quite naturally as we hold, display, or wear them as jewelry, and they transform, in ways we scarcely understand, negativity flowing into our lives from whatever source to positive energies. They radiate joy and healing as they catch light. Crystals also connect us with our angels and wise guides, a topic we will explore in Chapters 1 and 8.

Many people have tried to explain the wondrous properties of crystals. The ancient Greeks believed that all quartz crystals found on earth were pieces of the Crystal of Truth, dropped by Hercules from Mount Olympus, home of the gods. The Greek philosopher Plato (427–347 BC) claimed that stars and planets converted decayed and decaying material into the gemstones that were ruled by their mother star or planet. You will learn more of zodiac and planetary crystals in Chapter 8. To indigenous people throughout the world, including the Australian aboriginal and Native American peoples, stones and crystals are living entities, manifestations of the Great Creative Spirit, giving crystals the power to heal plants, animals, and people.

CRYSTAL HEALING

Crystals are an effective healing tool, not as an alternative to conventional medicine, but because in ways we can't fully explain, they kick-start our own immune system and generate our innate self-healing powers. They can speed the anticipated positive effects of pharmaceutical medicine, ease side effects of a necessary but debilitating treatment, and even when a patient is not responsive to formal medical intervention with a chronic condition, often bring relief from pain and anxiety.

Children are gifted crystal healers. For example, from a collection of different crystals even the youngest child will instinctively choose pink rose quartz or purple amethyst to ease a headache or yellow citrine for stomachache. This instinctive crystal knowledge is within us all, maybe carried in our genes, but logic and the everyday world make us distrust this innate wisdom. However, within a few weeks of using crystals in your everyday life, crystal wisdom spontaneously becomes accessible once more. You will often discover a crystal you choose purely by touch, even with your eyes closed, from a selection of many different kinds will ease a particular physical or emotional problem and is the one recommended over hundreds of years for the same condition.

Chapter 7 covers crystal healing, and healing is a theme that naturally recurs in most chapters.

WORKING WITH CRYSTALS

Crystals can be categorized in three ways: shape, kind, and color. If you are uncertain of the kind when you encounter a new crystal, its color and size will act as a reliable guide to its properties. Over the years you can collect different shapes, kinds, and colors of crystals so you have a comprehensive collection for every purpose.

If in doubt as to a crystal's meaning, hold the crystal between cupped hands and allow images, words, and impressions to come into your mind. These sensations will guide you to the best use of individual crystals. If unsure, ask yourself, "What does this crystal make me feel?" Instinct will then kick in.

SHAPE

ROUND crystals offer ongoing flowing energies and are ideal for every purpose.

POINTED crystals offer more powerful directed energies. Point the crystal inward to draw energy, healing, or protection toward you and outward to shed pain and negativity.

SQUARE or **RECTANGULAR** crystals bring stability and so balance an overactive home or workplace and absorb harm. (Wash them regularly under running water if you are using them protectively.)

OVAL crystals attract love and fertility, and bring abundance and happiness to families, children, and animals, releasing gentle healing powers however and wherever needed.

ELONGATED, BARREL, or **WAND-LIKE** crystals offer longer-term and slow-growing prosperity, career success, safe travel, and protection against ill-wishers. The wand shapes can be used to send a wish into the cosmos for yourself or others (pointed crystals were probably the original magic wands).

SPHERES, particularly clear quartz, energize and purify any room or workspace, attracting prosperity, health, and joy and transforming inertia, sickness, bad luck, or negativity into light and good fortune.

PYRAMIDS, especially the squat-shaped ones, are natural transmitters of healing and enhanced psychic powers and will bring peaceful sleep in a bedroom, and calm, unity, and harmony in the home or workplace.

KIND

QUARTZ, the most common mineral found on earth, brings change and energizes any person, place, or situation, the intensity depending on whether it is a soft or sparkling crystal.

JASPERS brings power and growth.

AGATES offer balance, protection, and stability.

FOSSILS slow down energies but bring wisdom and compassion.

VOLCANIC STONES, such as obsidian, cut through inertia and are fiercely defensive.

GEODES where tiny crystals are embedded in rock (a matrix) or, when split, reveal two halves of matching crystals heal any negative energies from the earth or contained in the land, remove spirits, and encourage the development of hidden talents.

COLOR

Consider both the actual color and the shade, whether clear and sparkling or a muted, cloudier hue. Some colors, such as red, orange, and yellow, are naturally hot and dynamic, while greens, blues, and purples are softer and calmer. To test this, hold a red stone in one hand and a soft green stone in the other. Almost immediately you will feel the dynamic, fast energies of the red and the slow, gentler flowing power of the green. I have a blind client who identifies the energies of a crystal purely by touch; as you develop this gift over time using the sensitive energy centers in your hands by a power called psychometry or psychic touch, it will enable you to instinctively *feel* the messages contained within different crystals. The following color listings give the notable qualities of the different color of crystals.

White, Bright, or Sparkling

Innovation and inventiveness, new beginnings, clarity, inspiration, developing talents, ambition, breaking a run of bad luck, good health, vitality, bringing or restoring prosperity when fortunes are low, and contact with angels and spirit guides. Can be substituted for any other color crystal in healing.

GEMS AND CRYSTALS: aragonite, clear crystal quartz, clear fluorite, diamond, Herkimer diamond, opal aura, rainbow quartz, white sapphire, white topaz, and zircon.

White, Soft, or Cloudy

The slower unfolding of potential, protection against negativity, fertility, pregnancy, mothers, babies and small children, restoring hope, success in writing and poetry, gradual new beginnings after loss, intuitive awareness, granting of wishes and fulfillment of dreams, and calling someone from afar.

GEMS AND CRYSTALS: calcite, howlite, milky opal, milky quartz, moonstone, pearl, selenite, and snow quartz.

Red

Action, courage, change, strength, determination, power, stamina, passion for any aspect of life, potency, victory, consummation of love, success in competitions, standing out against injustice, survival, and overcoming seemingly impossible odds.

GEMS AND CRYSTALS: blood agate, bloodstone/heliotrope, fire opal, garnet, jasper, red tiger's eye, and ruby.

Orange

Confidence, joy, creativity, fertility, abundance, inventiveness, independence, self-esteem, strengthening identity, happiness, and creative and artistic ventures.

GEMS AND CRYSTALS: amber, aragonite, beryl, calcite, carnelian, celestine, jasper, mookaite, and sunstone.

Yellow

Logic; focus; financial acumen, especially in speculation and technological expertise; communication; concentration; learning new things; examinations and tests, money-making ventures; adaptability and versatility; short-distance house moves or short-duration breaks; recovery through conventional healing, especially surgery; repelling envy, malice, and spite; and protection against those who would deceive.

GEMS AND CRYSTALS: calcite (yellow and honey calcite), chrysoberyl, citrine, jasper, lemon chrysoprase, rutilated quartz, and topaz.

Green

Love in every way and on every level, fidelity and commitment, growth and increase in any aspect of life, the acquisition of beautiful possessions, the environment, encouraging healthy plants and gardens, and good luck.

GEMS AND CRYSTALS: amazonite, aventurine, chrysoprase, emerald, fluorite, jade, malachite, moss agate, and tourmaline.

Blue

Idealism, traditional knowledge, justice, career and employment issues, especially getting a new job or promotion, leadership opportunities, authority, long-distance or long-term travel and house moves, marriage and partnerships of all kinds, expansion of business and financial improvement based on past efforts, and healing powers.

GEMS AND CRYSTALS: angelite, aqua aura, blue chalcedony, blue lace agate, blue quartz, celestite/celestine, cobalt aura, iolite, kyanite, lapis lazuli, sapphire, topaz, and turquoise.

Purple

Spiritual awareness and growth, imagination, meaningful dreams, teaching or counseling work, banishing what lies in the past but is still troublesome, contacting friends and family members with whom you have lost touch or who live far away, and protection (physically, mentally, emotionally, and psychically).

GEMS AND CRYSTALS: amethyst, ametrine, charoite, fluorite, lepidolite, sodalite, sugilite, super seven, and titanium aura.

Pink

Peacemaking, mending broken hearts, reconciliation and removing coldness or sorrows with family or in love, happy family relationships, friendship, gentleness and kindness, all matters concerning small or young animals, children and teenagers, especially girls entering puberty, women entering menopause, young or new love, the growth and regrowth of love and trust, and quiet sleep.

GEMS AND CRYSTALS: coral, kunzite, mangano or pink calcite, morganite, pink chalcedony, rose quartz, and tourmaline.

Brown

Stability, security, reliability, practical matters, the gradual accumulation and preservation of money, self-employment, learning new skills especially in later years, home, property, institutions such as banking, older people, animals, and conservation of old places and traditions, and finding what is lost or stolen.

GEMS AND CRYSTALS: banded agate, desert rose, fossilized or petrified wood, fossils, leopardskin jasper, rutilated quartz, all the sand-colored and brown mottled jaspers, smoky quartz, tiger's eye, and zircon.

Gray

Compromise, adaptability, maintaining a low profile in times of danger or unwelcome confrontation, neutralizing unfriendly energies, keeping secrets, and shielding against psychic attack.

GEMS AND CRYSTALS: Apache tear (transparent obsidian), banded agate, labradorite, lodestone, meteorite, silvery hematite, and smoky quartz.

Black

Easing necessary endings that will lead to new beginnings, banishing sorrow, guilt, destructive influences, acceptance of what cannot be changed, working within limitations and restrictions, blocking a negative or harmful force, and all psychic protection.

GEMS AND CRYSTALS: black coral, black opal, black pearl, jet, obsidian, onyx, snowflake obsidian, tektite, and tourmaline (schorl).

NATURALLY OCCURRING CRYSTALS

Traditionally our ancestors found crystals on local riverbanks, seashores, and hillsides. These were not tumbled or polished smooth, but glinted from within rock or needed to be cracked open to reveal their gleaming centers. If you keep your eyes open, particularly near water or where rocks have eroded, you may find your own treasures—especially jasper, quartz, and agate—that are in many ways even more potent than their polished sisters.

Each region and country has its local stones, and these are very potent, as they carry the earth energies unique to an area and so increase the normal properties of the crystal kind. Markets often have a crystal stall found locally, and you can buy nonprecious versions of emerald, opal, ruby, or garnet that are not as shiny but contain the same energies as the more expensive gem forms.

Wherever you go in your own country or around the world, buy samples of indigenous crystals and rocks, as these will not only contain the powers of the land but also retain your happy memories of your vacation. As you hold or wear them they will offer an instant source of joy rooted in the occasion you bought them on a special trip. Crystals absorb as well as reflect our energies and those of their native area.

MAKING A CRYSTAL REPOSITORY OF POWER AND HEALING

Buy any round, sparkling crystal, such as clear quartz, yellow citrine, a soft purple amethyst, or rose quartz, or use a favorite crystal pendant. If you cannot easily obtain a crystal, find a pure white round stone near your home.

Hold your crystal with open cupped hands to natural light outdoors, preferably when the sun is shining or toward the lightest part of the sky. This will fill the stone with optimism, energy, and power to attract good things into your life. As you do this, think of a time in your life when you were free, happy, confident, and powerful.

Leave your crystal in natural light either inside or outdoors until darkness falls. Then raise it to the moon or starlight outdoors. If it is a dark, moonless night, light a silver or white candle indoors and lift the crystal so the candlelight reflects into it. While doing this, picture a time when you felt safe and protected, and this will infuse your crystal with the power to safeguard you whenever you need protection. If you are using a candle, let it burn through or leave the crystal in moonlight or starlight until you go to bed.

The next morning, preferably near sunrise or when you wake, surround the crystal with white flowers in or outdoors. Recall a time when you felt strong, healthy, and fit, and this will fill the crystal with healing powers. Do not move the crystal until sunset so it absorbs the noonday and twilight energies.

Wear your crystal regularly or keep it near the center of your home where air and natural light circulate. Whenever you need one of the powers you have placed within your crystal, hold the stone between open cupped hands and ask for whatever you need. Place your hands so they enclose the crystal and feel the energies enter you.

Afterward, set it near greenery to reempower it with the energies of Mother Earth. You can reempower your crystal whenever you feel its powers weakening by setting it in front of a white candle and allowing the candle to burn through.

❖ 1 ❖

BEGINNING CRYSTAL EXPLORATION

FOR CRYSTAL WORK, WHETHER FOR HEALING OR attracting good fortune, love, or prosperity—or for being protected and getting answers to questions you may ask, whether from the angels or your own intuition—you will need a set of twelve similarly sized, tumbled (smooth polished) round crystals in different colors (see page 3). They should each be the size of a medium coin. The many uses for your twelve key crystals will be described throughout the book, and I will list other helpful crystals, so you will rapidly become a crystal expert.

Keep these twelve basic crystals in a bowl near the center of your home and pick one any morning you wish without looking, just by feel. Ask aloud or in your mind to be guided to a crystal for a particular purpose—for example, the confidence to speak clearly with authority at a crucial meeting at work. Alternatively, allow your hand to select the best crystal to give you the specific energies you need for the day ahead. The crystal predicts this, and again you will discover that this does reflect the events of the day ahead. Keep the chosen crystal with you during the day in a small drawstring bag or purse.

CHOOSING YOUR CRYSTALS

If you cannot obtain the twelve crystals listed starting on page 3, substitute one of the other crystals listed in the Introduction in the section on different colors. I recommend visiting a crystal store and passing your hand over a tray of crystals of similar colors and kinds to intuitively feel the ones right for you. However, you can buy crystals by mail order or online, as I will describe later how to cleanse and empower crystals to make them truly your own. Museums with a geological section often sell tumbled crystals as well as unpolished gems still embedded in the rock to display around your home or keep in your workplace.

YOUR TWELVE KEY CRYSTALS

Crystals are opaque, transparent, or translucent according to the density of color. Opaque crystals (for example, red jasper) have deep color and you cannot see through them. They absorb and powerfully transmit energies. Softer shades are gentler and slower acting. Sparkling transparent stones such as clear crystal quartz, through which you can see light, are lighter and livelier. Some contain lines or cracks within; all transparent stones are transformers of energy, though hazier pastel hues work more gradually. Translucent stones reflect shimmering light from the surface, such as brown gleaming tiger's eye. Translucent crystals amplify and reflect energies according to their intensity.

1. Clear Crystal Quartz, the Stone of the Life Force

The stone of the Sun, health, wealth, success, and happiness. This clear sparkling all-purpose crystal brings energy, good fortune, prosperity, joy, initiative, and new beginnings. Hold your clear quartz in the hand with which you write, wish for what you want most in the world, and then go out and make it happen.

When clear crystal quartz appears as your crystal of the day, be optimistic about the day ahead and maximize any opportunities that will almost certainly come your way.

2. Moonstone, the Crystal of Intuition

Shimmering translucent white or cream-colored, moonstone is the stone of the Moon in all her phases. Moonstone will cause unexpected advantages to turn up in your life, such as a twin soul crystal for meeting or developing love with a soul mate. This stone aids conception in those who are anxious or experiencing difficulties; children can use it to prevent nightmares, and it helps men as well as women to move into harmony with their natural rhythms and feelings. Moonstones protect travelers and commuters and bring the fulfillment of long-held dreams.

As a crystal of the day, the moonstone says trust your intuition. Beware of a less-than-open approach by others and of taking the path of least resistance.

3. Red Jasper, the Stone of Courage and Change

The stone of Mars, red jasper offers strength and stamina for busy times when you cannot rest. If anything is stagnant or moving backward, red jasper unblocks the obstruction and sets you back on the path to achievement. Use it for taking center stage, overcoming bullies, tackling prejudice or hostility head-on, and protecting against physical as well as emotional attack.

If red jasper is your crystal of the day, go directly for what you want and do not take no for an answer.

4. Orange Carnelian, the Crystal of Creativity and Independence

A crystal of Uranus, your gleaming orange carnelian fills you with self-confidence and fertility in the way you most need, whether to conceive a child, launch an artistic or literary venture, or express yourself creatively in some other form. Orange carnelian is excellent for self-employment and for the discovery of new interests and friends.

As your crystal of the day, carnelian indicates this is a good time for independent action, whether emotionally or at work. Do not undervalue yourself or accept second best.

5. Yellow Citrine, the Stone of Learning and Speculation

Sparkling yellow citrine is the crystal of swift-moving Mercury and will make you smile. Citrine brings success in learning new things and is called the merchant's crystal, promising that commercial speculation and business transactions, especially those involving buying and selling and studying of any kind, will be successful, as will matters involving communication and moneymaking ideas.

As your crystal of the day, citrine indicates you should communicate your ideas and needs clearly, especially at work. Try new activities, visit new places, and take chances rather than holding back.

6. Green Aventurine, the Stone of Good Luck

The crystal of Venus, green aventurine is a good luck charm and for this reason is called the gambler's crystal. Protective against accidents of all kinds, aventurine is excellent if you are always rushing round or have accident-prone kids. Kept at work, aventurine will help you come up with good ideas and positive solutions for ongoing problems. It is also the crystal of love and fidelity as well as gentle growth in every aspect of life.

As your crystal of the day, aventurine says everything you touch will work well and people will be especially cooperative; enter a competition or buy a lottery ticket.

7. Blue Sodalite, the Stone of Wisdom

Sodalite is the stone of the planet Jupiter, and it helps you speak wisely after considering your words carefully, rather than rushing into decisions or reacting impulsively to situations or people. Your sodalite will assist you to find and follow the life path that is right for you. It will make you a wise friend and adviser to your family and colleagues and ensure that you get the chance to take the lead in a matter or project close to your heart. Sodalite promises slow but sure steps up the career ladder as well as happiness in a partnership or marriage matters.

As a crystal of the day, sodalite advises checking all the facts and figures if matters seem uncertain. Look to long-term advantage rather than immediate results.

8. Purple Amethyst, the Stone of Balance

The stone of Neptune, gentle purple amethyst is the antistress stone and is called the all-healer. Amethyst will soothe people, animals, and plants and restore the energies of other overworked crystals (see page 9). It is also wonderful for getting rid of cravings, fears, panic, and anger at home or in the workplace. Amethyst is gently protective against noise pollution of all kinds, including technology and unfriendly ghosts as well as negative earth energies running beneath a home or workplace. It brings balance and reason to any situation, and it also brings quiet sleep and calm.

Amethyst as your crystal of the day indicates that you need to step back from conflict; listen to all sides of an argument but do not be pressured or rushed by other people's unreasonable demands or timescales.

9. Brown Tiger's Eye, the Stone of Gaining Advantage

Gleaming golden-brown tiger's eye is another crystal of the Sun and is a stone of financial and personal benefits coming into your life and growing, another good luck charm. Brown tiger's eye is an excellent crystal for entrepreneurs and people setting out in business for the first time and for building up a skill and knowledge base for a major future career change or self-employed enterprise. It also enhances artistic, performing, and creative arts, especially if you're aiming for fame and fortune. Tiger's eye reflects back all ill-wishing and envy.

As a crystal of the day, brown tiger's eye indicates you should look out for any chances to shine, make sure you claim credit for what you do, and do not listen to rumor mongers or those who try to involve you in their factions.

10. Pink Rose Quartz, the Stone of Kindness and Nurturing

Rose quartz is the good fairy crystal, another stone of Venus. It will attract peace at work and home and bring gentle, trustworthy love into your life, whether you're building a new friendship or relationship or increasing the love you have within your family or with someone special. Rose quartz is good for mending quarrels or coldness, and it relieves hurts from past unkindness or betrayal. Like amethyst, it brings peaceful and beautiful dreams; and like carnelian, it is another fertility crystal.

As your crystal of the day, rose quartz indicates you may need to keep the peace, either within your family or at work, but be sure you do not get blamed by both sides; good deeds will be repaid in the future.

11. Hematite, the Stone of Hidden Fire and Justice

This metallic shining gray stone, a crystal of Mercury and Mars, protects you against all harm and against those at home or work who drain you emotionally. Called the lawyer's stone, hematite brings justice in legal, official, and personal matters, as well as success in anything about which you are passionate. The crystal of inner fire, hematite brings out your talents at any age or stage in life. As a magnetic stone, hematite will draw success to you.

As a crystal of the day, hematite advises bringing matters that have been dragging on to a satisfactory conclusion; avoid being swept up in pettiness or emotional blackmail.

12. Black Onyx, the Stone of Protection

Gleaming black onyx, the stone of the planet Saturn, is the ultimate antipanic crystal, defusing dramas at home or in the workplace. Black onyx is good for clearing your mind if you need to make a decision and there are lots of conflicting opinions or pressures on you; it reduces overdependence on or by you, brings order to chaos, and calms hyperactivity, perfectionism, and pressure to do ten things at once. It also reduces the effects of bad influences and mind games on you or loved ones.

If this is your crystal of the day, resist anyone pressuring you to change your mind or make concessions; it is a day when truth and justice will prevail and secrets will be revealed.

CLEANSING AND EMPOWERING YOUR CRYSTALS

With crystals, however obtained, it is important to make them your own by removing the impressions of others who have handled them, empowering them with your energies, and programming them for particular purposes. Cleanse the whole set of crystals weekly and after intensive use, and cleanse an individual crystal that has been your crystal of the day during the evening after use. I have listed a number of methods for cleansing crystals in the following pages. The method you use depends on what feels right at a particular time for different crystals.

Cleansing a Crystal When You First Obtain It or After Use

Citrine, apophyllite, and kyanite are the only crystals that never need cleansing.

WATER

Wash crystals under a running tap. This works for most tumbled stones, except those that are fragile, like selenite, or metallic, like hematite. Leave the washed crystals to dry naturally.

AMETHYST

Make a circle of crystals around a large unpolished piece of amethyst for twenty-four hours as the amethyst will cleanse and empower them.

MOTHER EARTH

Rest your crystals on a small plate on the earth or in a large plant pot for twenty-four hours.

FRAGRANCE

Circle a sagebrush or a cedar smudge stick or a lemongrass, pine, juniper, frankincense, lavender, or rose incense stick in counterclockwise spirals in the air over any crystals to be cleansed for three or four minutes. Leave the incense to burn through near the crystals.

SOUND

Ring a handbell or Tibetan bells nine times or strike a small singing bowl over the crystals for about a minute. Repeat twice more until the sound fades.

LIGHT

Leave vibrant, richly colored, or sparkling crystals in sunlight from dawn (or when you wake) until noon. If the day is dark, light a white or gold candle where the light will shine on the candle, and leave it to burn through.

Place translucent, softly hued, or cloudy crystals in full or bright moonlight overnight or burn a silver candle to shine on them.

SALT

Leave crystals within a circle of salt or on a plate on top of a bowl of salt for twenty-four hours.

CRYSTAL PENDULUM

Pass a clear quartz or amethyst pendulum over a circle of crystals in slow counterclockwise circles nine times.

Blow three times very softly on an individual crystal as you hold it in your open cupped hands.

EMPOWERING AND PROGRAMMING CRYSTALS

You can empower crystals after cleansing. Hold an individual crystal in the hand you do not write with, and with the index figure of the other hand, press gently on top of the crystal until you feel a soft throbbing or warmth in your finger. Ask aloud or in your mind that the chosen crystal be used for the greatest good and the highest purpose. If it is to be used for a particular purpose, ask your guardian angels or Exael, Omael, and Othias, the angels of crystals and gems, to bless the crystal and name the purpose. To empower your set of twelve crystals, place them on a table in a circle and move the palms of your hands about an inch above the circle, the right hand making clockwise circles and the left hand counterclockwise at the same time for a minute or two, again asking the blessings of the angels.

CRYSTALS IN THE HOME AND GARDEN

CRYSTALS ENHANCE EVERYDAY LIFE BY ATTRActing abundance, happiness, and harmony into your home and protecting children and pets. You already have learned about twelve crystals you can use for many purposes, but at the end of this chapter I will introduce five additional crystals you can buy cheaply and easily that are especially related to the home and garden. These you can add to your set of twelve as crystals of the day.

Place crystals you like, either tumbled stones or those that are unpolished or still embedded in a rock matrix, around your home and outdoors or in plant pots in an apartment to protect your boundaries, family, and possessions from all harm, threats, and interference.

INFUSING YOURSELF, YOUR FAMILY, AND YOUR HOME WITH CRYSTALLINE COLOR

There are times when the energies of your home feel out of sync and everyone is lethargic or irritable and restless. This is because the aura or invisible energy field over the home receives impressions from the people who live there and who may bring stress home from work or school, from the energy fields of neighbors and visitors and the land on which your home is built.

Even the smallest crystal will gradually over months fill the atmosphere with calm or joy, but if you, family members, or the home need a quick burst of energy or harmony, try this. You can also do this before a social gathering at home to create a beautiful atmosphere and after people have left to clear the buzzing energies and restore the house to peace.

Specify what you need from the crystal color—for example, calm for yourself or restored happiness to the home after a quarrel. Pick a crystal from your set by feel with your eyes closed, passing your hands above them till you are drawn to one. You will tune into the crystal most needed at this time, and if the color is surprising, your natural intuition assisted by your guardian angels have picked up underlying factors and energies not consciously recognized that need fixing. So the crystal you select will always be the right one.

If you are fixing the home, stand as near the center of the home as you can. Place the chosen crystal between your cupped open hands a few centimeters from your face and slowly and gently inhale through your nose, visualizing crystal light of the color of the stone. *Feel* the light flowing through every part of your body, soothing if it is a cool color, like blue, and energizing if it is a warm shade, such as red. If the color is needed for yourself, exhale a slow sigh through your mouth, visualizing dark smoke-like rays of stress, anxiety, or exhaustion leaving your body.

If you are doing this ritual for another family member (that person does not need to be present), a pet, or a specific room or the whole house, picture in your mind the source for which the color is needed. In this case, blow softly out through your mouth three times, visualizing the person, animal, or place suffused in the crystalline light. Whether you're sending color to yourself or another target, continue the sequence in a slow, steady rhythm, picturing the crystalline color enclosing you or the target in a sphere of protective, relaxing, or empowering light. You can do this anywhere, even quite subtly while traveling or at work, by holding the crystal between closed cupped hands or touching it in a pocket or bag to make the spiritual connection.

MAKING YOUR CRYSTAL HEART OF YOUR HOME

To make your home harmonious, filled with the life force that brings abundance and repels harm, whether you're in a studio apartment in a rented house or a remote three-story dwelling, create a crystalline oasis as near to the center of your home as possible. Within even a few days of establishing your crystal place, mealtimes, whether alone or with family, will become more pleasurable, difficult family members will be more communicative and friendly, and plants, animals, and people will thrive.

Best of all, the presence of crystals in your home over the months and years spontaneously regulates and balances the flow of energies, so you become luckier and healthier and enjoy better relationships within and outside the home. You do not need to buy all these crystals I suggest at once or indeed more than one or two for each purpose, but you can add ones you like over the months and the years. Once you start collecting crystals, I guarantee it will become a lifetime passion.

You will need:

- A low table surrounded by comfortable seating.

- Small white candles, one for each family member, including absent ones and, if you wish, departed loved ones. Light these after dark or as each person who lives with you returns, and then burn candles for absent or deceased members with a silent blessing.

Set your bowl of twelve crystals near the center of the table, plus any additional ones as you learn about them or to which you feel attracted. Put tiny crystal angels in a circle, one for each family member. Crystal angels will be discussed on pages 32 and 96, and you have the alternative of using their zodiacal crystal in the form of an angel or even as an additional crystal (see page 96). Alternatively or additionally, add a small bowl of angel crystals (discussed on pages 32 and 96). Also, in the center, set a clear quartz crystal sphere, to constantly transform negative or stale energies into harmony and radiate as light and as positive luck, health, and prosperity, attracting energies.

Add a small amethyst geode with tiny sparkling amethysts in rock to absorb any negative energy from the earth beneath your home and to radiate calm and balance.

Have also a small rose quartz sphere or pyramid on the table to attract and keep love and loyalty in the home and to transform unkind words, sibling rivalry, or intergenerational squabbles into kindness.

Add greenery and potted plants (not cut flowers, as growing ones spread the life force better), and if you wish, burn gentle floral oil or have dishes of rose- and lavender-based potpourri to help stir and balance the energies.

Whenever you have time, sit quietly, either alone or with family members, by candlelight, with only the sound of soft background music. Electronic devices are a no-go in this space. Children can experience a calm quiet end of the day by candlelight and so go to bed relaxed and happy. Adults can also finish the day in quiet contemplation if alone or in conversation rather than working on projects from their offices, letting in the outside world through the computer or iPad, or watching television until falling into a fitful sleep. Crystalline slow-down time is the best cure for insomnia and stressing over the day at two a.m.

INTRODUCING BACKGROUND CRYSTAL ENERGIES TO YOUR HOME

For harmonious mealtimes, keep on the dinner table a dish of very small blue lace agate crystals, green jade, green or blue calcite (polished or natural), blue Andean opal, blue chalcedony, and green or purple fluorite, or a mixture of any of these.

Hang clear crystals on cords at windows to draw in rainbows and so joy, health, and abundance from all directions into your home. You can buy ready-made sun catchers, but ensure they are real crystal and not glass.

If the stairs face the entrance to your home, crystals suspended above doors leading off even a tiny hallway spread light and positive energies and encourage the life force to flow upstairs and not to drain straight out of the front door.

Place a small dish of vibrant crystals, such as gold-and-blue lapis lazuli, glowing orange or yellow amber, fossilized tree resin that often has fossilized insects or leaves, green amazonite, golden chalcopyrite, golden rutilated quartz, and rainbow iridescent bornite or peacock ore, near the front door.

If you need a sudden input of enthusiasm before you leave in the morning for a potentially challenging day, hold one of the crystals to which you are drawn for a minute or two and breathe in the energy—or take it with you along with your crystal of the day.

Touch a vibrant sparkling crystal, such as clear quartz, orange carnelian, or citrine, when you want to be noticed socially on a date or special occasion or shine at work, and again, take it with you in a small bag if you wish.

Have darker crystals in a dish also by the front door—for example, black obsidian (volcanic glass), jet, Apache tear (obsidian through which you can see light), or smoky quartz—so you can pick one on your return from work and allow it to absorb the tensions of the day. These are also good for repelling and reducing the effects of nasty neighbors or hostile visitors. Hold the dark crystal for a minute or two until you feel tension draining away, and later wash it and leave it to dry naturally.

If your home feels out of balance because of a spate of illness, frequent quarrels, or unpleasantness from neighbors, or if you feel spooked by a paranormal presence in the home, amethyst crystals, especially geodes (tiny amethysts embedded in a rock matrix) are naturally protective. Set these on a window ledge in every room (you only need tiny ones) or add a few extra amethysts to your main dish of crystals—if you need new beginnings, use a chevron amethyst that also has white in it. Before placing them, hold each between your palms and say, *Be protection for my home and all who live within it against negativity and transform darkness to light.* Once a week, pass a lighted lavender incense stick over each amethyst in counterclockwise and then clockwise spirals, and this will cleanse and reempower them.

Keep three or four jadeite in a bowl of water to permeate fresh living energies through the home or workplace.

CRYSTALS AND YOUR GARDEN

Keeping crystals in your garden, on a balcony, or in an indoor plant area will increase the health of the plants and at the same time amplify the health- and wealth-attracting energies of plants to spread throughout the home and family. The Chinese made miniature crystalline gardens that represented a pathway that might temporarily offer a glimpse of paradise. The miniature gardens were often made of jade, a stone associated with immortality.

Gardening crystals include blue and green moss agate and green and white dendritic or tree agate; green chrysoprase; green jade; green and often darkly patterned jasper; any banded agate; green, blue, or purple fluorite; green calcite; and golden rutilated quartz. Gardening crystals protect home, property, and land from intrusion, harm, vandalism, or theft and from difficult or noisy neighbors.

Set a moss or tree agate in the pot of a thriving green plant on either side of your front door so that only positive people and energies will enter your home when the door opens.

Plant six small green jade or rutilated quartz crystals in a pot of basil, thyme, or mint or beneath a bay tree in order that prosperity, health, and happy love relationships will grow as the plant grows.

Mark the boundaries of your home with any four gardening crystals (you can mix the kinds if you wish). Set above them protective plants such as bamboo, cactus, bay trees, palms, myrtle, juniper, hawthorn, or rowan trees.

Bury a gardening crystal at the four corners of your land or, if you're in an apartment, put them at the four corners of the home in plant pots in which you have planted herbs. Protective herbs include basil, cumin, lavender mint, parsley, rosemary, sage, thyme, and vetivert. Hold each crystal in turn before planting and say, *May the guardians of this land keep my home and loved ones safe from all physical, psychological, and psychic harm and danger from false friend and from stranger.*

If a particular plant or tree is wilting, circle a gardening crystal over the plant and around all the leaves or the trunk, first counterclockwise nine times and then clockwise nine times, asking Mother Earth and the essence of spirit of the plant or tree to send blessings and strength into its roots. Do this daily until the plant improves.

Energize water for watering flowers or plants by placing a green jade in the water for two or three hours beforehand.

Keep a small jade in the bottom of a cut flower vase for prolonged flower life.

FIVE HOME AND GARDENING CRYSTALS

You can add these crystals to your essential set of twelve.

1. Blue Lace Agate

A stone of Jupiter, veined with white or threads, which is often associated with angels, is a natural background crystal for calming stress. This stone encourages clear communication; take it with you when addressing a meeting, going for an interview, or speaking in public or in front of the media to be clear, concise, and persuasive, and to avoid tripping over words. You can carry it to negotiations for achieving compromises, especially with tactless, critical, or overassertive people; it is an excellent anti-aggressive or anti–noisy neighbor stone. For difficult colleagues or visitors, soak three blue lace agates in a jug of water for an hour or two, remove, and use the water for making drinks for them to soften harsh or critical words.

As a crystal of the day, blue lace agate says you should express what you feel quietly and firmly and you will receive a favorable response. You may need to teach or advise others, so be patient.

2. Green Calcite

Green calcite, a stone of Venus, whether polished and tumbled or natural and looking like green ice, slows workaholics and people who are always in a hurry, brings harmony to mealtimes and social gatherings, attracts money and opportunities through hard work, and especially favors new businesses. It is also good for healthy eating regimes and for anyone who has food issues or phobias. It calms overactive or clumsy children and hyperactive, noisy animals; it also encourages generosity and sharing. Sacred to the earth and earth spirits, green calcite encourages healthy plant growth and environmental awareness.

As a crystal of the day, it says that temporarily you may be asked to give more than you receive, but this extra input will bring future rewards; if money is short, see if you can juggle resources or earn some extra through a hobby, for better times are coming.

3. Rutilated Quartz

Clear quartz filled with gold, silver, or red rutile needles is sacred to the Sun, and it restores balance at home and minimizes tantrums from drama kings and queens of all ages. The crystal of hidden gold and hidden talents, it is one of the best crystals for enhancing inner beauty and for developing and making money from creative arts and crafts, music, writing, and performing in public. It attracts the right job to people who are unhappy at work or have been made redundant. It is also useful for training and retraining, especially in the second half of life. It can help you overcome ageism and recover after redundancy. Often referred to as angel hair, each rutilated quartz crystal contains a guardian spirit who will protect the owner or user from harm.

As a crystal of the day, rutilated quartz says you should reach for those seemingly impossible dreams, for you are far more talented than you realize. Push yourself forward and shine.

4. Tree or Dendritic Agate

Another stone of Venus, this white crystal has feathery-green tree-like inclusions or veins. This is a crystal of slow-growing prosperity and is an excellent networking crystal in the workplace, online, and overseas. It is also good for conducting group activities and bringing people together in a common cause or interest, finding or reconnecting with lost or estranged relatives, dating successfully on the Internet, growing your own business, and turning an interest into a moneymaker.

As a crystal of the day, tree agate says cooperate with others and work on joint ventures; accept that matters may be slow in progressing but have assured success.

5. Jade

Usually green, though it can vary from white to lilac and yellow or black, jade comes in two forms, nephrite jade and jadeite. Called the gardener's crystal and the crystal of gradual growth in all things, jade belongs to Venus. Jade brings good fortune in life and in games of chance, and it is a natural increaser of prosperity if kept in the cash register or near an accounts computer in a business. Jade is a crystal of new and young love and love in old age, and it promises this love will be lasting. Food vessels were made of jade in old China to transfer the life force and health through the food eaten from them.

As a crystal of the day, jade says now is a time to think about your longer-term future and consider making a commitment, decision, or investment you have been putting off; save rather than spend today.

❧ 3 ❧

CRYSTALS, LOVE, AND HAPPY FAMILIES

CRYSTALS, BECAUSE OF THEIR VIBRANT POWER, can be used as a focus to call to us what will make us happiest, whether that's love, fertility, the safety and well-being of our children and pets, or all of these. Look at the end of this chapter for more crystals to add to your collection, including those that are related to the themes of this chapter.

CRYSTALS AND LOVE

Gems and crystals have traditionally been given as love tokens throughout the ages. Even today each wedding anniversary has its own gem (see page 104 for full list), For example, the second wedding anniversary is garnet, the twelfth is jade, the thirtieth is pearl, the thirty-fifth is emerald, the fortieth is ruby, and the sixtieth is diamond.

Crystals and gems preserve love through the years, but they also have the power to draw love, whether they're worn in the form of a pendant, a ring, or a bracelet, or as matching twin crystals in a drawstring bag, one for each lover. Increasingly, people who are divorced or who are alone choose a favorite love stone and wear a ring on their wedding finger to mark they are complete within themselves.

Love crystals work by opening our personal energy field or aura that surrounds us as we empower and then wear the stones. Gems empowered for love will spontaneously not only increase our natural radiance but also call to us the person who is right for us and draw us seemingly by chance to the place where, usually totally unexpectedly, we meet our true love.

What is more, we can program a crystal to increase commitment, to persevere when the going gets tough, or even to bring about reconciliation. You can also program a gem or crystal to give to a lover. The crystal-empowering ritual that follows is based on calling a love known or unknown but can equally well be adapted for commitment, or for the preservation of love in difficult times or for reconciliation, by changing the words slightly.

Empowering Your Crystal or Gem for Love

Light a green candle, the color of love. Look into the flame and say, *I light this candle to call and keep the love of* (name if known) *or the person who is right for me.* Pass the jewelry in a clockwise direction three times around the candle flame and say just once, *I call you, my love, to come to me and stay with me, faithfully and lovingly, as long as the sun shines and the waters flow over the earth, which is forever.* Blow out the candle, saying, *Come to me, my love, and stay with me forever.* Wear the jewelry whenever you go out on a date, to a place where you hope to meet someone new, or at times in your life when you need it—for example, to increase commitment. Repeat weekly, using the same candle until it will no longer light, then replace it.

Love Crystals and Gems

Here are some crystals and gems that can be used for love.

You can buy non–gem quality rubies, emeralds, and garnets that work as well as the more expensive jewels.

Orange amber protects against negative outside influences and interference, and it calls a twin soul and/or a former love from our youth. Purple amethyst heals love quarrels and prevents obsessive love and codependency. Pale blue aquamarine calls an estranged love back, and it helps two people with different lifestyles live together in harmony. Orange carnelian rekindles passion that has faded in an otherwise loving relationship; it is good for commitment when matters are slow moving. Diamond brings fidelity and defense against love rivals or those who try to break up a long-term relationship. Emeralds hidden near your heart attract love in later life. Worn openly, they can heal a relationship after infidelity or separation. Green garnet makes secret or forbidden love accepted by others; red garnet brings romance and fun into a love weighed down by worry. Green jade should be used for new love, gentle love, and fidelity. Red jasper is for passion and overcoming a jealous ex-partner. Twin creamy moonstones are given, one for each partner, to keep love new, especially if the relationship is long distance. Blue and green moss agate can be used for love growing from friendship or with a work colleague. Pink rose quartz is good for love after an earlier destructive relationship and for reconciliation after quarrels. Pearls should be given to a new bride so she will never cry during her marriage. Ruby is for mature and lasting love; it becomes paler if love is untrue, and it prevents anger between partners. Blue sapphire is used for new love, commitment, and fidelity, especially if one partner regularly works away from home. Golden topaz traditionally is worn to attract a wealthy lover. Green and pink unakite, the stone of Mars and Venus united, is a twin soul crystal.

CRYSTALS AND FERTILITY

To conceive a child, whether by natural means or through medical intervention such as IVF, place one of the fertility crystals listed on page 31 on an indoor window ledge during the crescent to the full moon. Oval stones or small crystal eggs are ideal.

On the night of the full moon, prick the crystal with a tiny silver pin prior to lovemaking. Leave the crystal and pin on the ledge until noon the next day, then wrap them in white silk; keep in a drawer until the next crescent moon when the ritual can be repeated if necessary.

As a variation, a rounded amber and pointed jet crystal can be put in a red cloth bag, tied with three red knots, and placed under the bed during lovemaking.

Another old method of conception is to place a green and pink unakite beneath your pillow before lovemaking.

Fertility Crystals

Orange amber can be used for potency and fertility, especially if you are anxious after prolonged artificial contraception. Orange carnelian is best for older mothers-to-be. Creamy moonstone is the most powerful fertility crystal. Shimmering white selenite jewelry worn in the weeks before you try for a baby brings your body into harmony.

Crystals in Pregnancy and Childbirth

If you or your partner is pregnant, choose any crystal to which you are instinctively attracted, or one of the fertility crystals, when you first feel the baby kicking inside. Hold the crystal on the womb whenever the parents talk or sing to the unborn child and take it to the labor ward to encourage the baby to be born easily and safely (this is good for elective caesareans as well as natural births).

After the child is born, keep the crystal near the infant's cradle; circle the special birth crystal over a fretful baby to soothe him or her.

Selenite induces calm through pregnancy, childbirth, and all the stages of motherhood; it's also a lovely gift for a new grandmother.

CRYSTALS AND CHILDREN

Children are naturally in tune with crystal energies. Once they are old enough to use crystals without the risk of swallowing them, give your child a bag of small round different-colored crystals of their own with which they can play, weave stories, and heal their dolls and teddy bears. Traditionally mothers would create an amulet of protective coral or jade to hang over the infant's sleeping area, and amber teething rings are back in fashion.

Present a crystal for a newborn baby, whether given at a naming ceremony or christening or when you first visit the parents and newborn. Before giving the crystal, endow it with a special talent or blessing for the child, fairy godparent–style. Add crystals to the collection for each birthday or significant milestone, such as starting school; when the child leaves home he or she can take the crystals as a link with home.

Crystal Protection and Children

Many children, especially sensitive ones, suffer fears, nightmares, and night terrors, and a protective crystal set by the bedside and activated by the child each night can help overcome fears of the dark or of ghosts or human intruders.

Sometimes instead of a traditional bedtime story, allow your child to choose a crystal from his or her bag, and together weave a story of the crystal angel or fairy. Place the crystal near the child for quiet sleep and peaceful dreams. Set large, unpolished pieces of pink rose quartz or purple amethyst as nighttime protectors. Alternatively, buy a crystal fairy or angel.

Older Children and Crystals

If a child or teenager is being bullied, empower a small red or orange crystal chosen by the child to be carried to school or college in a small pouch or purse or as a luck bringer if tests or examinations are a problem. Empower the crystal by lighting a white candle and passing the crystal round it nine times clockwise, asking the angels specifically for the protection or support needed by your child. Blow out the candle and reempower it weekly.

Sew a small protective crystal from those in the next section in the lining of a child's coat.

A jar of pearls in a child's bedroom brings the guardianship of the children's Archangel Gabriel of the Moon while he or she sleeps. Add a few clear quartz (the stone of the Archangel Michael of the Sun) for protection by day.

Crystals That Are Especially Good for Children

Blue angelite with veinlike wings connects children with their guardian angels; it's also good for establishing sleep rhythm in babies and young children. Deep blue-and-gold lapis lazuli helps gifted children who are frustrated at school and is good for those with communication problems. Banded agates prevent accidents and calm temper tantrums and teenage angst. Green and black malachite protect teenagers from making unwise Internet contacts or being bullied by text or e-mail. Red tiger's eye can be used against playground or out-of-school bullying; also, this stone prevents an older child being tempted by peer pressure into unwise behavior. Pink-and-white chalcedony eases jealousy and sibling rivalry; it also accustoms babies to the world after life in the womb. Rose quartz is useful for healing fears, phobias, trauma, and abuse, and for bringing quiet sleep. Mangano, or pink calcite, relieves fretfulness in babies and small children, especially when unwell; it is good for a mother and child to bond after a difficult birth and for small children to overcome fears of animals or strange places. Purple amethyst can be used for children of any age with sleep problems or nightmares or who suffer from anxiety; it guards psychically sensitive children and adolescents from unfriendly ghosts and paranormal happenings. Citrine is a useful stone for study and retaining knowledge; it blends together stepfamilies and a new marital partner. Jade protects a child against illness and harmful people; mother of pearl, placed on a newborn infant's stomach for a few seconds, endows the babe with the love and protection of the mother even when she is absent.

CRYSTALS AND ANIMALS

Because crystals are such a powerful part of nature, they reconnect even the most urbanized pet with the earth, restoring health and vitality and reducing snappishness or hyperactivity.

Whatever kind of creature shares your living space, leave small dishes of mixed green, brown, golden, and orange crystals around the home near where the pet usually sits or sleeps. Unpolished minerals or those embedded in rock are most tuned into earth energies.

Soft-green jade crystal, placed in pet water for a few hours before use (remove the crystal before drinking) maintains health and soothes an aggressive or boisterous pet or one that sprays its territory.

Turquoise fixed to pets' collars, to the bridles of horses, and to the mirrors of caged birds prevents theft or the creature getting lost or straying. Turquoise is also a charm against accidents, the malice of animal haters, and the ill effects of harmful pollutants. If you adopt an animal from a rescue center, unpolished chunks of rose quartz and green calcite near the entrance to your home persuade the animal to stay.

Crystals That Are Especially Good for Pets

Brown, pink, and fawn banded agates can be set beneath the corners of the bed for older or chronically ill pets. Blue aquamarine relieves shock and trauma in badly treated animals and maintains the health of fish if placed in a tank or pond. Dark green bloodstone with red spots can be used for successful animal breeding, as it prevents new mothers rejecting their young and assists timid creatures to resist bullying by older animals. Cat's eye as yellowy green chrysoberyl, grayish green or yellow cat's eye quartz, or green tiger's eye keeps cats safe, particularly if they roam at night or live in busy areas. Dalmatian jasper, with black spots on a fawn or cream background, keeps dogs in good condition and reinforces obedience training. Pale brown and roughly textured desert rose protects lizards, snakes, hamsters, and guinea pigs, as well as very old and sick creatures of all kinds. Green glass-like fluorite attracts birds, dragonflies, and butterflies to the garden. Gleaming blue hawk's eye guards all creatures during travel and away from home; it is also health-giving for cage or aviary birds. Snowflake obsidian is very healing for horses when being exercised where there is traffic.

FIVE CRYSTALS TO ADD TO YOUR COLLECTION

These are five more crystals especially relating to love, fertility, children, and animals that you have the option of adding to your collection.

1. Amber

Amber, stone of the Sun, contains the power of many suns and the souls of many tigers and so brings confidence, increased charisma and radiance, and quiet courage to make your unique mark on life and to love yourself as you are. This translucent golden-orange, yellow, or brown fossilized tree resin removes obstacles you put in your own way, improves short-term memory, melts rigid or confrontational attitudes in the workplace, encourages spontaneous recall of past lives, and helps trace your family ancestry.

As a crystal of the day, amber promises unexpected admiration and even flirtation, but think before giving up reliable love for momentary passion.

2. Unakite

Ruled by Pluto, planet of endings of what is no longer wanted and new beginnings, olive-green and salmon-pink unakite makes you prioritize and work systematically if you are overwhelmed by tasks or demands on your time; encourages harmonious partnerships, both in love, coalitions, and joint enterprises in business; is especially helpful if you are working with a relation or friend; and gives knowledge of the location of what is lost. Carry unakite when taking calculated risks and making wise investments. The crystal of happy lasting relationships, unakite is traditionally placed in a sealed cloth bag as a marriage or commitment symbol; replace it every seven years and throw the old crystal into running water.

As a crystal of the day, unakite advises focusing on future opportunities and not past mistakes or losses; and it helps you avoid making old mistakes.

3. Turquoise

Blue-green mottled turquoise is the stone of Jupiter, the supreme stone of leadership, authority, promotion, justice, and equality. It relieves jet lag and fears of flying. It is protective if you or family members suffer prejudice or bullying; it also overcomes writer's or artist's block. Turquoise is a stone of clear communication when you are giving information or suspect you are been fed misinformation.

As a crystal of the day, turquoise says you should clear up misunderstandings and should avoid people who try the hard sell or emotionally pressure you.

4. Malachite

Emerald green with black stripes, malachite is another stone of Pluto and is the ultimate antipollution crystal; it discourages overreliance on others. Keep malachite near freezers, refrigerators, microwaves, televisions, computers, and game consoles and with your mobile phone overnight. Malachite counteracts overbright fluorescent lighting and nasty negative phone calls and e-mail messages. It also overcomes fear of flying.

As a crystal of the day, malachite suggests you resist possessiveness or energy draining by others and follow your own path.

5. Banded Agate

This earthy crystal, called the earth rainbow, with concentric bands of color, predominantly gray, black, or brown, is the stone of Saturn. It overcomes unrealistic or unrequited love and increases chances of winning competitions of physical strength and endurance. It is the ultimate antishopaholic crystal when carried in a purse or wallet.

It balances families that come together through remarriage and between different generations as well as different factions and groups that need to work together. It is good for coping with two jobs and transforming creative ventures into a marketable form.

As a crystal of the day, banded agate tells you to consider both sides of a question and try to discover hidden factors you have not considered; work and act at your own pace today.

CRYSTALS
AND THE
WORKPLACE

THROUGHOUT THE AGES, CRYSTALS, ESPECIALLY sparkling clear ones such as citrine and clear quartz or richly colored stones like blue and gold lapis lazuli, were thought to naturally attract moneymaking opportunities. In fact, they can be used today to guide you—seemingly spontaneously—to the right places and people who will assist you in your career. Carrying or wearing your workplace crystals will increase their power, as they harmonize with your personal energy field over the weeks and months.

The single most effective workplace crystal is a clear crystal sphere, which integrates people and situations when kept in the center of an open-plan office or factory floor for harmonious, productive teamwork. In an individual workspace, set it near a telephone or on top of a computer or fax machine to bring in advantageous business calls, sales, and Internet networking. It will also transform negative energies filtering into your aura.

ATTRACTING WHATEVER YOU MOST NEED IN THE WORKPLACE

If you are applying for a job in a difficult economic climate, launching a new business, or seeking promotion when there is fierce competition, you can add further power to your workplace crystal. Work over a seven-day period. With a paper knife, scratch into the wax of an unlit blue candle, *New job be mine* or *Bring deserved promotion.* Adapt the words to what you most need in the work field. Set your workplace crystal in front of the candle. A blue and gold lapis lazuli, turquoise, or dyed-blue howlite crystal is ideal for a major venture, and a yellow citrine is suited for swift action.

Light the candle and say the words you scratched on the candle aloud seven times. Now pass the crystal seven times around the flame, repeating the words again seven times.

Blow out the candle and carry or wear the crystal. Repeat the empowerment on the next six days having relit the same candle and placed the same crystal in front of it. Do this from days two through six. Blow out the candle each day, and on day seven leave it to burn through.

PROTECTION IN THE WORKPLACE

The most effective way of gaining ongoing crystalline protection in the workplace is to empower a dark crystal to place on your desk or in your workspace. If you drive a lot in connection with your job, keep the crystal in the glove compartment of your car or van.

The best protective workplace stone is black obsidian, volcanic glass, and if there is a nasty atmosphere at work, use an obsidian arrow pointing outward. Blue goldstone, dark blue glass with golden glints like a starry sky, is another powerful workplace guardian and, like obsidian, will also attract success and recognition to you.

Every morning before work or driving, hold the crystal between your open cupped hands. Blow three times gently on to the crystal, and after each breath, say, *Be a shield for me to block out negativity, malice, and hostility. Allow only light and harmony to pass through.* Each day, name any particular stresses, situations, or people from which you wish to be shielded and any special wishes or tasks to be fulfilled by the end of the day. Set the crystal in your workspace. Wash the crystal weekly under running water and leave it to dry naturally.

WORKPLACE ISSUES

If you suffer from psychological bullying at work, an increasing problem, set a dark green-and-red bloodstone between you and the bullies. Put one near the phone or computer if you work for a call center or have to regularly deal with difficult phone calls or complaining e-mails; circle it round the phone or computer counterclockwise if a call or e-mail is confrontational.

Use yellow jasper to counteract spite, jealousy, and lies and those who would damage your reputation. Place five of these in a small dish in your workspace or in a drawstring bag in your drawer to stop colleagues gossiping about you; leave them inside your desk or locker when you have a day off to extend this protection in your absence.

Buy two or three small clear quartz crystals with the points at one end that you can set along the three outer sides of your workstation. Turn the points of the crystals outward when trouble or intrusion appears on the horizon. If you have the points of the crystals facing inward the rest of the time, the crystals will transmit positive energies toward you during the day.

Blue calcite deters cliques, factions, and workplace rivalries, and it protects equipment, possessions, and premises from theft and the workplace from dishonesty.

Green and black malachite crystals will guard you from the more adverse effects of modern equipment. Have one at each of the four corners of your computer or any technical machine you regularly use.

If you cannot display your crystals because of the nature of your work, keep rounded ones in a drawstring bag.

Use orange carnelian to protect you against accidents if you operate machinery or are involved in utilities, building, or construction industries.

CRYSTALLINE BALANCE IN THE WORKPLACE

Westernized elemental balancing is an easier method than feng shui and is just as effective, unless feng shui is naturally part of your tradition.

Ideally all four of the ancient magical elements—earth, air, fire, and water—should be represented in a workplace and space, though in differing proportions according to the nature of the business or your career. Following are the elemental associations for different careers and workplaces. Having a dish in your workplace of any of the three or four crystals associated with your job is the best way of ensuring the elemental mix remains and is balanced.

Earth

All these careers and workplaces benefit from the use of Earth crystals or where there is an excess of Earth with the counterbalancing Air crystals.

EARTH CAREERS AND WORKPLACES

Day-care center workers, caring for older people and the disabled, animal welfare and veterinarians, animal trainers and communicators, sculptors and potters, midwives, bankers, accountants, tax inspectors, house sales agents, government officials, land and property surveyors and developers, craftspeople, all who care for their families full- or part-time, house renovators, painters and decorators, factory workers, funeral directors, family-run businesses, forestry and environmental workers, farmers, bakers, the food industry, wood carving, carpenters and furniture makers, gardening, and mining and minerals.

QUALITIES IT BRINGS TO THE WORKPLACE: stability, commonsense, practical skills, systematic approach, gradual increase in prosperity, realism, awareness of limitations imposed by time and resources, loyalty, flow of regular work and orders, patience and perseverance, attention to detail, and tolerance.

CRYSTALS: most agates, amazonite, aventurine, emerald, fossils, jet, malachite, moss agate, obsidian, rose quartz, rutilated quartz, smoky quartz, tiger's eye, tree agate petrified wood, and all stones with holes in the center.

EXCESS: inertia, sluggishness, stinginess with money from a usually generous person, obsession with details, inability to grasp the wider picture, unwillingness to consider alternative approaches, obsessiveness with tidiness, excessive homemaking or nest building, pessimism, and territorial tendencies.

TO COUNTER: increased Air.

Air

All these careers and workplaces benefit from the use of Air crystals or where there is an excess of Air with the counterbalancing Earth crystals.

CAREERS AND WORKPLACES

Architects, town planners, doctors, pharmacists, dentists, psychologists and psychiatrists, all sales and shop workers, mortgage advisers and financial advisers, students, anyone in the communications industry from mobile phone sales to newspapers and magazines, speech therapists, public speakers, detective or investigative work, transport workers and drivers, travel agents and resort representatives, all who work with the Internet, software designers, television engineers, radio and phone engineers, solicitors, judges, fitness instructors, publishers, authors of factual books, teachers, researchers, dancers and choreographers, musicians, explorers, scientists, computer programmers, and fixers.

QUALITIES IT BRINGS TO THE WORKPLACE: logic, clear focus, an inquiring and analytical mind, ability to communicate clearly, concentration, versatility, adaptability, multitasking, curiosity, commercial and technological acumen, moneymaking abilities, ingenuity, sales and marketing skills, and ability to work under pressure.

CRYSTALS: amethyst, blue lace agate, citrine, clear crystal quartz, danburite, diamond, lapis lazuli, sapphire, sodalite, sugilite, and turquoise.

EXCESS: being super critical, sarcastic, or witty at the expense of others, unusually rushed or inaccurate work, incoherence, unwillingness to explain thinking or ideas, crankiness, gossiping, being liberal with the truth, poor timekeeping, losing data or forgetting appointments, and changing the focus midway without reason.

TO COUNTER: increased Earth.

Fire

All these careers and workplaces benefit from the use of Fire crystals or where there is an excess of Fire with the counterbalancing Water crystals.

The performing and creative arts, chefs, cooks and kitchen staff, firefighters, the armed forces, jewelers and photographers, security workers such as the police, car mechanics, car manufacturers, inventors, geniuses, poets, artists, interior designers, ambulance workers, all rescue service personnel, anyone in the theater or performing arts, heads of companies and directors, central heating engineers, troubleshooters, anyone connected with fuel industries or production such as gas, oil, petrol, or electricity, blacksmiths and metalworkers, those who work in animal slaughter, butchers, radiotherapists, and anyone in the nuclear industry.

QUALITIES IT BRINGS TO THE WORKPLACE: creativity, originality and fertility of ideas, enthusiasm, inspiration, leadership, breadth of vision, courage, generation of enthusiasm in others, transformation of raw ideas into a marketable creation, ability to see possibilities in even unpromising situations or projects, and willingness to accept when work is leading nowhere and to jettison unproductive ventures.

CRYSTALS: amber, blood and fire agate, bloodstone, boji stones, carnelian, desert rose, garnet, hematite, iron pyrites, jasper, lava, obsidian, ruby, and topaz.

EXCESS: irritability and impatience, temper tantrums, being autocratic, forcing an unrealistic work pace for self and others, sudden loss of interest in a project, inability to switch off from a subject or from work, becoming increasingly accident-prone, empire building, carelessness with property, unnecessary risk taking, inappropriate sexual remarks or jokes, and inflaming dormant office passion.

TO COUNTER: increased Water.

Water

All these careers and workplaces benefit from the use of Water crystals or where there is an excess of Water with the counterbalancing Fire crystals.

WATER WORKPLACES AND CAREERS

Social services, the export trade, alternative medicine and therapy, nurses and therapists, mental health workers, psychotherapists, play therapists, beauty and fashion consultants, florists, all who work in the water industry or hydroelectric power, fishermen and sailors, counselors, writers of fiction and children's books, customer service advisers, clairvoyants and mediums, the hotel and hospitality trade (also earth), those who produce or sell alcohol, laundry workers, cleaners, refuse disposal workers, plumbers, swimming instructors and those who work in or maintain swimming pools, glassmakers and glaziers, and ministers of religion.

QUALITIES IT BRINGS TO THE WORKPLACE: intuitive understanding, empathy with and sympathy for others, negotiation and peacemaking skills, imagination, ability to work with others, gentle good humor, uncanny power to anticipate the needs of a situation and thoughts of other people, openness to new ideas and opinions, willingness to deputize for others, acceptance of people for what they are and not for their status, and networking skills.

CRYSTALS: aquamarine, calcite, coral, fluorite, jade, kunzite, milky quartz, moonstone, opal, pearl, selenite, and tourmaline.

EXCESS: becoming overemotional about a professional matter, being manipulative, playing favorites, role taking (e.g., helpless little girl/big sister/dad knows best), attention seeking, flirting, constant need for reassurance/praise, excessive socializing/"you're my best buddy" syndrome, instigating rivalries, jealousy, and oversensitivity to constructive advice.

TO COUNTER: increased Fire.

Changing the Elemental Mix

On occasions the mix will need to be altered. Elemental excesses can occur quite spontaneously in the workplace and result over time in an unusually high number of stress-related absences, factions developing, or even resignations and unease.

RESTORING IMBALANCES

If your office seems out of balance (for example, everyone is unreasonably irritable), use some balancing crystals listed in the previous section to subtly correct the balance. One or two of the needed balance elements are sufficient when added to your crystal dish. Keep a set of one or two of each of the elemental crystal kind in a drawer or locker to replace any existing crystal in the dish as required. You will instinctively know how many to add to rebalance.

You can also soak an elemental crystal in water for a few hours and use the crystal-infused water in juice, tea, or coffee for people around you. Keep a small bottle of an appropriate balancing water to drink or splash on pulse points. Old mineral-water bottles are ideal.

CRYSTALS TO ASSIST SELF-EMPLOYED BUSINESSES

If you have a store or warehouse or hospitality business, guide business into your company premises by placing two pointed clear quartz crystals hidden on either side of the door or gate, slightly pointing inward, and then use more pairs at regular intervals, always hidden and pointing inward to mark an invisible pathway of energy to guide people into and around your premises. In a store, put two hidden pointed crystals, again pointing inward, in the two front corners of the shop window. Imagine the way a customer would walk past displays or toward individual tables to eat, stopping finally at the cash register, and use hidden crystals to direct their feet and gaze.

Set extra crystals on either side of the invisible path pointing toward any special displays where you would like customers to pause and continue all the way to the register.

Keep a dish of smoky quartz near safety equipment, such as a fire extinguisher, to protect work premises from fire, flood, cyclone, earthquake, malice, and ruthless competitors and intruders, and to shield your computers against virus attack.

Set one in the glove box of your company vehicle to guard from theft and mechanical breakdown and protect the driver against road rage.

Keep a sparkling yellow citrine called the merchant's stone in a cash register, and if you have a new business, display the first dollar bill you earn.

CRYSTALS THAT ARE ESPECIALLY GOOD FOR ATTRACTING OPPORTUNITIES IN THE WORKPLACE

Banded agate is good for restoring financial stability after losses, for getting bank loans, and for stability in a workplace where jobs are under threat. Green amazonite is useful for women starting a business or wishing to do well in male-dominated professions. Gold chalcopyrite can help in starting a second business or expanding a business; it is also used for getting a promotion in a long-term career plan. Green chrysoprase will help in finding a first job and obtaining work in a difficult climate. Yellow citrine brings swift commercial success, especially through financial speculation and talking your way into the right job. Purple fluorite reduces unnecessary pressure in the workplace to stay late and take work home. Herkimer diamond is useful for aiming for the top, being a leader, and making money through company share schemes. Use black jet for overcoming business-debt problems, getting an overdue salary increase, establishing a second career after retirement, and finding the right business premises. Lapis lazuli can help facilitate successful interviews and tests. It is good for careers involving travel and for organizing functions, conferences, meetings, and seminars. Creamy moonstone is a friend to shift workers and those whose jobs involve constant traveling and irregular hours, as well as workers with disabilities. Green and blue moss agate, as well as tree agate, helps family businesses and Internet companies and is used for training that may take years. Use rutilated quartz for successful career changes, for finding work after redundancy, and for a more spiritually or creatively focused career change. Older workers can carry rutilated quartz to adapt to change, especially new technology.

FIVE WORKPLACE CRYSTALS TO ADD TO YOUR COLLECTION

These are my five favorite crystals for office harmony and career success, if you wish to add them to your collection.

1. Bloodstone/Heliotrope

A crystal of the Sun, dark green bloodstone with red or orange spots and sometimes white markings, is a stone of courage to stand against individuals and organizations who seek to intimidate you and for young people who are bullied on social-networking sites. It is protective in an overcompetitive workplace or if you are pressured to achieve unrealistic targets. Keep a bloodstone in a glass pot of loose change where natural light shines on it to attract money to your home or business. It is lucky for any sports competitions or matches, whether you compete or gamble; it helps human and animal mothers bond with their children after traumatic births.

As a crystal of the day, bloodstone says you should stand your ground and persist politely until you get what you want, no matter how great the odds against you.

2. Green Chrysoprase

This stone of Venus, apple green or mint green, is a fertility crystal, especially if a second baby is slow to follow the first. It breathes life into a relationship after a major setback, betrayal, or outside interference. Rub one over the envelope of any applications or letters you send out relating to employment, money, or new business; hold one over a computer mouse before applying online for a new job or business finance.

As a crystal of the day, chrysoprase says that a new opportunity when least expected and from the least anticipated source could move you out of an impasse and open new future avenues.

3. Fluorite

Purple fluorite, a stone of Neptune, is a natural calming, de-stressing, and focusing crystal so that dreams and ideas can be expressed in a practical way in the workplace; it slows down hyperactive adults and children so they can achieve their goals systematically and helps workaholics avoid burnout. It is good for spiritual businesses, such as therapists and healers who make a living from their gifts. It raises the ethical and spiritual level in a very commercial, dog-eat-dog, or materially orientated workplace. For children and adults who do not feel at home in the world to value their uniqueness, fluorite is an exceptionally useful stone.

As a crystal of the day, purple fluorite says that what you want may not seem the most financially viable option, but you should not compromise your principles.

4. Lapis Lazuli

Blue-and-gold–flecked lapis is the stone of wise Jupiter. Around the home, lapis encourages family loyalty. Lapis inspires the trust of others, especially when you have to deputize for a senior. It encourages steady career advancement and is the best crystal for gifted children and those with autism or Asperger's; it is a stone associated with the accumulation of wealth and property and attaining stardom through the performing or creative arts. Use this stone when seeking justice through official channels.

As a crystal of the day, lapis lazuli says you may be called upon to take the lead or have a chance to further your ambitions. Rise above pettiness and attempted double-dealing.

5. Obsidian

Stone of Mars, black volcanic obsidian helps everything run smoothly, from organizing the company office party to executing a multimillion-dollar project. It is protective against those who take advantage and against con artists; use for a fierce defense against aggressive people or in a fight for compensation from a big corporation or government body.

As a crystal of the day, obsidian says you have more power than you realize that you can use if you are not afraid to challenge an outmoded status quo.

CRYSTAL AMULETS FOR PROSPERITY, GOOD FORTUNE, AND SAFE TRAVEL

IN EARLIER CHAPTERS YOU EMPOWERED CRYSTALS for many purposes, including love, fertility, and career. These are called amulets, symbols that store power and/or protection that can be released over a number of weeks or even months and years.

Talisman is the term used when you empower a crystal for a particular purpose and time frame (for example, to study successfully for and pass particular examinations in six weeks' time).

A charm bag is a collection of crystals kept in a drawstring bag, whose individual powers and meanings combine to create an ongoing focus for any positive purpose.

EMPOWERING YOUR CRYSTALS AS AMUETS AND TALISMANS

Select the crystal or crystals best for your need, from those listed in the different chapters. Light an incense stick, such as lavender, rose, or frankincense, and write in the air a few centimeters above your crystals your specific needs and any timescale, using the incense stick like a smoke pen. Say the words aloud as you write them. This imprints your words on the ether, the magical space in which wishes can be transformed into reality. By touching the crystal or charm bag and saying the words in your mind in the days ahead, you can release the powers into your life at any time.

If the matter is ongoing, once a month on the night of the full moon, leave the crystals on an indoor window ledge all night to pick up the full moon energies. Later in the chapter, I describe how you can combine different crystals in a charm bag to mix and match the protection and powers you most need.

TRAVEL CRYSTALS

Travel is one of the main purposes for which we may need a protective crystal amulet or charm and the following crystals are especially effective.

Kunzite and Sugilite

The car driver's and commuter's friend, purple-striated kunzite and dense purple-and-black sugilite kept in a vehicle glove box can prevent road rage, stress in heavy traffic, accidents, and overtiredness on long journeys; it can also calm difficult passengers and reduce travel sickness.

Sodalite

Dark-blue-and-white sodalite overcomes fears of flying. Add a small one to a bottle of water to drink or splash on pulse points during takeoff and landing and when experiencing turbulence; alternatively, wear one as a pendant and touch it when you get scared.

Smoky Quartz

Carry a brown or gray smoky quartz when you travel alone late at night or in a crowded, potentially dangerous area. Breathe in the misty gray and exhale your fear as dull red light to act as a shield and lower your profile so you will be less visible to hostility.

Turquoise

Turquoise or its less expensive cousin, dyed-blue howlite, covers all travel eventualities, protecting adventurers of any age, guarding against picking up bugs and infections in countries where hygiene is basic, preventing pets and small children from straying while in transit and children from getting hurt, and avoiding travelers falling foul of local laws and customs.

Especially Good for Safe and Happy Travel

Green amazonite is best for going on adventure vacations, camping, or visiting dangerous parts of the world; it is also used for riding a bicycle to work. Clear blue or green aquamarine is helpful for journeys by sea, cruises, and long-haul travel. Blue aventurine helps avoid travel disruption and the loss of luggage, passports, and currency. Hawk or falcon's eye (blue tiger's eye) or any cat's eye crystal stops you from getting lost while driving, especially at night, or being conned on vacation; and it keeps backpackers or gap-year students safe. Green jade prevents illness on vacation for solo travelers and older travelers. Blue or yellow moonstones prevent jet lag when crossing time zones. Red tiger's eye protects you against drunks or drug addicts, especially on trains and late-night buses. Golden-orange sunstone is good for happy vacations, obtaining the resources to travel, and successfully relocating abroad.

PROSPERITY CRYSTALS

To attract money into your life, especially if you have money worries, on your crystal table set a dish of clear quartz crystals mixed with citrine (seven in total: four yellow citrine and three clear crystal quartz). Put the dish where candlelight will shine on the crystals and burn a yellow candle next to it weekly; hold the crystal dish to the candlelight and say seven times, *Gold and silver I have none. Into my life good fortune comes—and quickly until finances improve.*

Golden Tiger's Eye

Tiger's eye brings both gradual and sudden urgently needed resources and stops a drain of resources. Use tiger's eye to start and maintain an ongoing money pot to ensure resources continue to flow into your home long term and to encourage saving.

Place a tiger's eye in a small ceramic pot, like a sugar bowl, with a lid. Add a gold- or silver-colored coin every day; keep the pot in a warm place to symbolically incubate wealth. When the pot is full, put the money into a savings account; leave the tiger's eye in the pot as you build the coin collection again.

Cat's Eyes

Yellow or greenish cat's eyes are incredibly lucky financially as well as protective against malice and envy. People often wear the same cat's eye for years so it grows in strength and good fortune; traditionally, it is bought or ordered on Wednesday, Thursday, or Friday.

Especially Good for Attracting Prosperity

Amethyst reduces the tendency to overspend, gambling addictively, and make unwise investments. Polished gold chalcopyrite brings a large infusion of money through the sale of treasures you find in markets, garage sales, or your attic. Bronze and gold-flecked goldstone attracts unexpected money through a bonus, a rebate, or a gift. Metallic silvery iron pyrites brings solid financial advantage, deters the user from making unwise financial decisions, and is a natural reducer of debt. Pearls symbolize prosperity from small beginnings. Start with a single pearl and each time you have a small success, add to your pearl collection to build up the energies. A small green peridot in your purse or wallet with credit cards will draw in money, and one with your mobile phone, iPad, and computer will deter pickpockets and muggers.

CRYSTALS FOR GOOD LUCK

You may already have a particularly lucky piece of jewelry, and this can be empowered weekly to increase its luck-bringing abilities. The more you carry it or wear it, the stronger its luck-bringing energies become.

Your own zodiac- or birth-sign crystal is especially lucky, and these I have listed in Chapter 8 on personal crystals.

If you have experienced a period of bad luck, light a dark-colored candle and a white one. Set the crystal, whether one from the following list or one personal to you, in front of the white candle. Sprinkle a pinch of pepper in the dark candle flame and say, *Misfortune be gone.* Sprinkle salt in the white candle flame and say, *Burn bright and light the way to good fortune.* Blow out the dark candle and leave the white one to burn through.

Tourmalated Quartz

A clear quartz with threads of black crystal within, tourmalated quartz changes bad luck to good luck generally and can be used in the empowerment mentioned previously. Tourmalated quartz should be carried in a white bag or purse when specific good luck is needed.

Rainbow Crystals

Any crystal with a rainbow sheen, such as black rainbow obsidian or clear quartz with rainbows reflecting inside, is a wish crystal. Rainbow obsidian turns around bad fortune in career or business.

Hold five tumbled stones in your closed cupped hands, shake vigorously five times, toss, and catch them, saying, *Bad fortune be gone.*

Rainbow quartz promises happiness and the restoration or increase of fortune in the way you most need it; hold it to the light so the rainbows reflect and make a wish.

Especially Powerful Bringers of Good Fortune

Red-and-green bloodstone is best for any sports competitions, training, or matches; keep this in your sports bag or sewn in the lining of a lucky garment. Dark-blue goldstone with gold flecks, the stone of all performers and creators, brings a lucky break or good contract; touch your blue goldstone under the stars and visualize your big chance materializing. Bronze goldstone is a lucky charm for competitions, games of chance, and the lottery; use the same goldstone or goldstone jewelry as its powers accumulate. Green jade reverses bad fortune, whether in love, money, or career, after a spate of accidents or illness. Green jasper brings deserved compensation after unfair treatment. Smoky quartz guards against misfortune caused by the ill-wishing of others, curses, and hexes. Staurolite, the gray or black stone with an embedded equal-armed cross, is a traditional protective luck bringer (carried by the former US president Theodore Roosevelt). Yellow sunstone carried with a moonstone ensures good luck and protection against misfortune by day and night.

MAKING A CRYSTALLINE CHARM BAG

Charm bags, which can contain three, five, or seven crystals that can be the same crystal for extra power or a combination of different crystals, offer ongoing good fortune and protection against bad luck. Use a small drawstring fabric bag or a purse.

Green is the luckiest color, but you can also make charm bags for prosperity (yellow for fast results and blue for slower and lasting wealth), for travel (green), for love (pink or green), and for fertility (orange). Check the color meanings in the Introduction. Some crystal mixes are traditional in charm bags. However, you can use any combination of crystals for specific purposes.

Three small green-and-white amazonites and three green aventurines in a small green purse or drawstring bag attract good luck to any games of chance, lottery entries, competitions, or any form of speculation. Keep the crystals with any tickets or competition entries.

Make a lucky charm bag with three amazonites, a little dried basil, and mint. Leave the bag in front of a turquoise candle until the candle burns down. Keep the bag near the computer for online lottery or contest applications and for luck in online dating.

Keep seven olive-green olivine or her darker sparkling bottle-green gem sister peridot in a green charm bag for ongoing prosperity and to ensure you are never defrauded.

Carry five tiger's eyes in a gold or yellow charm bag when dealing with stocks and shares, considering property investments, or meeting someone who has made you an offer—touch the charm bag in your pocket and you will *know* if the offer is good or too good to be true.

Assembling the Bag

Light a candle in the same color as the charm bag and place your chosen crystals in a dish in front of the candle. You could combine different crystals for an all-purpose bag—for example, turquoise for safe daily travel, jade for lasting love and good fortune, a rainbow wish crystal so your dreams will come true, goldstone for unexpected good fortune, and smoky quartz to protect you from ill-wishing. You can make bags for family members.

If you wish, add your zodiac crystal (see page 96) or that of the person for whom the bag is intended. As you hold the crystals in your open hands to the candlelight, name three times the purpose of the bag, who the bag is for, the timescale, and say, *May only goodness and light fill these crystals.* Add each crystal to the bag separately, naming its specific purpose or, if they are all the same crystals, repeating the purpose of the bag.

Empowering the Bag

Close the purse or tie the bag with three knots and set it in front of the candle. Light two incense sticks in any floral or tree fragrance from the candle. Taking an incense stick in each hand, with the incense stick you are holding in the hand you write with, move it clockwise and the other stick counterclockwise a few centimeters over the bag, in a steady, gentle rhythm over the crystals. When you feel the crystals are full of power, blow out the candle and leave the incense in holders to burn though either side of the bag.

Keeping Your Bag Powerful

Once sealed, your bag should not be opened. If the bag is for someone else, give it to him or her as soon as possible after the making. Name it for that person if you cannot give it for whatever reason, and keep it with a photograph of the person or even a pet. In addition, you can create very small charm bags to carry with you in a handbag or pocket or keep in the glove compartment of your car—for example, a bag of mixed kunzite and fluorite. Or in luggage, you might keep a bag with mixed sodalite, blue chalcedony, and red tiger's eye. Carry your bag at crucial times (for example, before an interview).

FIVE CRYSTALS TO ADD TO YOUR COLLECTION

Here are five more crystals I have introduced in this chapter. You have the option of adding them to your collection. It does not matter how many or few crystals you use to pick your crystal of the day; the right energies will always be revealed.

1. Amazonite

Blue, green, or turquoise amazonite is the woman's power stone and assists women, especially those who are alone, in maximizing their potential and all women in overcoming bullying relationships at home or work. Amazonite is lucky for men and women winning prizes through luck and merit.

Nine small amazonites in a circle in your workspace will attract new business and new orders if you're self-employed, or will bring you promotion and independence if you are working within an organization. It is good for female-focused businesses.

As a crystal of the day, amazonite says you will be able to overcome ongoing prejudice or injustice and obtain the respect and consideration you deserve.

2. Blue Goldstone

This beautiful blue and gold sparkling glass stone resembles a starry night sky and says we can achieve anything by our own efforts since the stone is a thing of beauty created by humans. Blue goldstone is the stone of actors, actresses, all performers, and any involved in theater, publishing, art, or the media to attain stardom. The crystal of shift workers and those who travel at night, blue goldstone prevents our repeating old mistakes and patterns. Above all, blue goldstone is a wish stone. Breathe into a goldstone or goldstone jewelry on a starry night and whisper your wish into it.

As a crystal of the day, blue goldstone says seize opportunities with both hands, for you are all set to make a big impression.

3. Goldstone

The bronzed red and gold original version of this magical stone, goldstone reduces chronic self-consciousness that makes socializing, eating, or speaking in front of others painful. A luck and money bringer, goldstone helps you make a living from selling your talents and your creations. It is a transformative stone for turning life around by no longer pleasing others or trying to fit in but by loving yourself as you are and for who you are.

As a crystal of the day, goldstone says that you should relax, have fun, and not worry what others are thinking of you.

4. Iron Pyrites

Metallic silvery iron pyrites with natural holes as tumbled stones is very protective against control freaks, unfair criticism and manipulation by a partner, parent, or employer. Keep iron pyrites near the computer or phone for filtering scams. The stone is a reminder not to accept second best nor follow the easy path. Iron pyrites returns negative thoughts and psychic attacks to the sender, and it improves memory and concentration.

As a crystal of the day, iron pyrites says that a seeming bargain or perfect offer could be the answer, but check carefully for flaws or hidden conditions.

5. Sunstone

Golden-orange sunstone with a sparkly iridescent sheen is the stone of pure happiness, and it generates enthusiasm if you are surrounded by negative people. Carry sunstone when starting a new sports or exercise regime to give you the impetus to persevere. Keep sunstone by your computer if advertising your services online or to increase the positive effects of your profile on a social networking or dating site. Sunstone reduces overdependence on the approval of others.

As a crystal of the day, sunstone promises good times ahead; enjoy the present without worrying if happiness will last (it will).

CRYSTALS FOR HEALTH, HAPPINESS, AND WELL-BEING

ONE OF THE MOST IMPORTANT ROLES OF CRYStals is their ability to naturally create and maintain a sense of health, happiness, and well-being in our lives.

USING CRYSTALS AND COLORED CANDLES TO INDUCE CALM AND PEACEFUL SLEEP

Candles in the same color as a crystal amplify its effects. If you feel stressed and unable to switch off or relax, crystals and candles restore your inner rainbow so you spend the rest of the evening calmly and go to bed pleasantly sleepy.

On your crystal table, make a circle of crystals of the main rainbow colors: red, orange, yellow, green, blue, and purple. In the center of the circle, set a larger clear white crystal. Behind each crystal, light a small candle of the same color. Sit comfortably facing the rainbow. Visualize the colored rays from the different crystals and candles and the central white crystal ray, becoming a slowly turning, moving wheel of light, surrounding you and enclosing you above in a rainbow bubble. As you inhale slowly through your nose and exhale through your mouth, *see* the rainbow colors merging into white and golden light and entering your body, rising from your feet and at the same time pouring in from above and all around you so your bubble now is white and gold. Close your eyes and feel the warm tingling of the white and gold, saying in your mind or softly aloud over and over, *I am pure light.* Gradually you will connect with your breathing once more. When you are ready, open your eyes and spend the time before sleep listening to gentle music. Some people use soft music throughout.

CRYSTAL LAYOUTS OR GRIDS FOR WELL-BEING

You can create a layout of crystals around yourself, your bed, your chair, or a room; around food, drink, or utensils; around your computer or work tools; or around a photograph of a person or a place where you need peace. Reread the previous chapters to see the many different ways crystal layouts can be used. They are limited only by your ingenuity and imagination.

Initially use a set of nine small pink rose quartz or purple amethysts for bringing calm and balance and a second set of clear quartz or warmer yellow citrine for energizing. Over time, buy nine crystals in red, orange, yellow, green, blue, purple, pink, brown, gray, and black. These you can mix and match in your crystal layouts or grids.

AN ALTERNATIVE METHOD OF MAKING CRYSTAL WATERS

If you want a detailed list of crystals that are safe to soak directly in water, check my books *The Complete Crystal Handbook* or *The New Crystal Bible*.

AVOID SOAKING DIRECTLY: azurite, cinnabar, copper in any form, crocoites, anything containing erithyrite or fuchsite, halite, lapis, malachite, meteorite, selenite, turquoise, or vandanite.

This second spiritual elixir creation method is just as effective as soaking. Half-fill a large glass bowl with water, and in it float a heavy, small open glass container in the center of the bowl or a sealed small glass container (like an old makeup jar with a screw-top lid). Hold each crystal in turn, adding one at a time to the smaller floating container, stating the purpose for which you are making the elixir. Leave the bowl near a window that catches a lot of light for twenty-four hours. Fill bottles with the small container water for use.

Using Crystal Waters

Add crystal water to baths, wet a flannel with crystal water, or add crystal water to shampoo or shower gel in a shower. Splash crystal elixir on your hairline, brow, throat, and inner wrists (carnelian, amber, or clear fluorite are best) to refresh you during the day if you feel tired, pressured, or lethargic.

Massage elixir into aching limbs or joints (orange or yellow aragonite) or on the brow and temples to relieve headache (rose quartz) and blue lace agate or aquamarine into the base of your throat to express your ideas and feelings clearly but without being confrontational. Use the elixir for shining healthy hair (moonstone) and for mouth rinses to freshen your breath (citrine or chrysoprase).

Make tea, coffee, or cold drinks for anyone present using just a few drops of any blue or green crystals infused water if tensions or tempers rise at home or work.

To reduce stress left over from work and insomnia, make bedtime drinks with purple fluorite or jade water.

Sprinkle smoky or rutilated quartz crystal–infused water around your home or workspace to protect yourself from sarcasm, gossip, spite, or bullying (amazonite if you are a woman).

Add elixir to the rinse cycle of your washing machine to infuse the clothes you or your family will be wearing the next day with energy (chrysoprase)or with good luck (green aventurine). Use any blue or yellow stone elixir for memory or concentration or to create a good impression. Alternatively, sprinkle a few drops on the garments before you iron.

If you're on a diet or trying to give up smoking, drink amethyst or ametrine water throughout the day to reduce cravings or waning moonstone elixir to help lose weight and lessen food-related anxieties.

For fertility, massage your womb with moonstone water before lovemaking and on the three nights before and the night of the full moon.

Add protective and energizing crystal waters (aquamarine and yellow jasper mixed) when washing a car or motorbike, and sprinkle a protective mix and a calming mix (rose quartz and jade) over children's play equipment, bicycles, and jungle gyms to prevent fights and accidents.

Bless a new home, workplace, or vehicle with angelite, chrysocolla, and aventurine mixed in a crystal elixir.

Sprinkle rainbow or snowflake obsidian elixir crystal water around or on any items you have bought or have been given, especially if they were owned previously or have unknown origin.

Fill a plant-watering pump spray bottle with mixed jade, blue lace agate or strawberry quartz, and rose quartz crystal elixir to lighten the atmosphere of a room or spread a sense of well-being before a gathering or after a quarrel.

Put rose quartz or emerald water on your wrists and pulse points to attract or increase love.

FIVE CRYSTALS TO ADD TO YOUR COLLECTION

These are five extra crystals that are especially good for health and well-being that you have the option of adding to your ever-growing collection of crystals.

1. Ametrine

This natural mix of purple amethyst and sparkling yellow, citrine, ruled by Mercury, is the crystal of balance and as such is ideal in jewelry or as an amulet if others around you are overemotional or changeable. The negotiator's crystal, ametrine breaks barriers between two dramatically different viewpoints, and it eases returning to work after a break.

As a crystal of the day, ametrine says you will make a breakthrough in bringing two warring factions together and so make life easier for you.

2. Lemon Quartz

This lemon-yellow clear crystal, ruled by Mercury, is the ultimate detoxifier both physically and emotionally. It brings good fortune and new people and interests into your life, repels spite and vicious words if you have to see a jealous or malicious person regularly, and breaks the hold of a manipulative person or someone who plays mind games.

As a crystal of the day, lemon quartz advises staying detached from an argument between friends or family, as you may end up being blamed in a sudden about-face by the combatants.

3. Snowflake Obsidian

This black obsidian with white spots or small white flower shapes, ruled by Saturn and Mars, makes us value ourselves for who we are now rather than trying to fit into impossible images of perfection. Bury snowflake obsidian outside the front door to prevent misfortune through loss of money or illness or love; it positively releases pent-up anger or resentment in order to move relationships and self forward.

As a crystal of the day, snowflake obsidian says that you may discover someone you did not like or trust is reliable; express old sticking points in a new way.

4. Rhodochrosite

Rose pink with white or paler pink banding, ruled by Venus, rhodochrosite brings movement after a period of stagnation or doubt and regeneration of enthusiasm and purpose; it is helpful for children starting child care, school, or college so that they will find friends easily and settle in. A calling-back crystal, rhodochrosite can help you find a lost lover, a friend, a family member who has broken off all contact, or a missing pet.

As a crystal of the day, rhodochrosite says open your heart to the possibility of love and friendship, and you may find that it was close to you all the time; choose old valued friends rather than exciting new acquaintances.

5. Ruby in Zoisite

Green and dark pink to red ruby in zoisite that is ruled by Venus and Mars combines passion for anything or anybody with gradual practical growth energies of the earth. Good for same-sex couples and gender issues, ruby in zoisite helps restore passion in a relationship if one partner is having sexual difficulties or is contemplating infidelity. It is also useful in the workplace for meeting deadlines and avoiding unwise passions flaring in harmonious male and female relationships.

As a crystal of the day, ruby in zoisite says you may need to balance your desire for immediate results with the safer but duller path of waiting and seeing.

SENDING HEALING THROUGH CRYSTALS

CRYSTALS HAVE BEEN USED IN HEALING SINCE ancient Egyptian times. While they are not intended as a substitute for conventional medicine, crystals trigger our self-healing and immune system into action and boost the positive effects of conventional treatments.

HEALING WITH YOUR PERSONAL SET OF CRYSTALS

Your personal set of twelve crystals is ideal for healing, as you will have already formed a strong spiritual connection with their energies.

Before using crystals for healing, ask that the healing archangels, Raphael, Ariel, Zadkiel, and Gabriel, send their blessings through the crystals in the way and time that is right for all.

Afterward, wash the crystals under running water or spiral the smoke of a floral or tree incense stick over them, thanking the angels.

The following list gives you the healing significance of different colors. You can create a second extra set of crystals for healing if you choose. Keep these in a special healing bowl made of glass or ceramic.

Choose one crystal in all the main colors listed and two for white—one sparkling and the other with softer energies. Some conditions respond to more than one color.

White Sparkling

HEALING POWERS: whole body healing; general health; integration of mind, body, and soul; brain; neurological disorders; autoimmune system; and acute pain relief.

GEMS AND CRYSTALS: aragonite, clear crystal quartz, clear fluorite, diamond, Herkimer diamond, opal aura, rainbow quartz, white sapphire, white topaz, and zircon.

White Cloudy

HEALING POWERS: hormonal disorders, breast or womb problems, fertility, pregnancy, childbirth and mothers' and babies' fluid balance, gradual recovery from illness, depression or exhaustion, and bone marrow and white-cell disorders.

GEMS AND CRYSTALS: calcite, howlite, milky opal, milky quartz, moonstone, pearl, selenite, and snow quartz.

Red

HEALING: stimulates the entire system, energy, strength, raising low blood pressure, improving circulation, cellular growth, blood ailments (especially anaemia), reproduction and fertility, feet, hands, skeleton, back, uterus, penis, vagina, and impotence.

GEMS AND CRYSTALS: blood agate, bloodstone/heliotrope, fire opal, garnet, jasper, red tiger's eye, and ruby.

Orange

HEALING: ovaries, small intestine, spleen, gallbladder and bile (also yellow), kidneys, coeliac conditions, menstruation and menopause, arthritis and rheumatism, weight and food-related issues, and immune system.

GEMS AND CRYSTALS: amber, aragonite, beryl, calcite, carnelian, celestine, jasper, mookaite, and sunstone.

Yellow

HEALING: stomach and liver, food allergies, digestion, lymphatic system, metabolism, blood sugar, memory and concentration, nervous exhaustion, smoking, jaundice, and eczema and skin problems, stimulates the nervous system.

GEMS AND CRYSTALS: calcite (yellow and honey calcite), chrysoberyl, citrine, jasper, lemon chrysoprase, rutilated quartz, and topaz.

Green

HEALING: heart; lungs; respiratory system; ulcers; infections and viruses, especially influenza, bronchitis, pneumonia, fevers, and colds; panic attacks; addictions; asthma; and hay fever and airborne allergies.

GEMS AND CRYSTALS: amazonite, aventurine, chrysoprase, emerald, fluorite, jade, malachite, moss agate, and tourmaline.

Blue

HEALING: thyroid gland, throat, fevers, inflammation of the skin and mouth, teeth, childhood rashes, tumors, cuts, bruises and burns, pain relief, lowers blood pressure and pulse rate, eyes, ears, migraines and headaches, diabetes, communication difficulties (especially autism, Tourette's and Asperger's), and speech disorders.

GEMS AND CRYSTALS: angelite, aqua aura, blue chalcedony, blue lace agate, blue quartz, celestite, cobalt aura, iolite, kyanite, lapis lazuli, sapphire, topaz, and turquoise.

Purple

HEALING: headaches and migraines, scalp, hair, sinusitis, all mucous problems, addictions (especially alcohol abuse and gambling), neuroses and phobias, hyperactivity and ADHD, sciatica, childbirth, nerve endings and connections, psychological disorders, the separate hemispheres of the brain, and the entire nervous system.

GEMS AND CRYSTALS: amethyst, ametrine, charoite, fluorite, lepidolite, sodalite, sugilite, super seven, and titanium aura.

Pink

HEALING: glands, stress migraines, ear problems, psychosomatic and stress-induced illnesses, babies' and children's illnesses, psychological trauma and abuse (especially left from childhood), female hormonal and reproductive issues from puberty to menopause, and sleep disorders and nightmares.

GEMS AND CRYSTALS: coral, kunzite, mangano or pink calcite, morganite, pink chalcedony, rose quartz, and tourmaline.

Brown

HEALING: feet and legs, bowels, large intestine, illnesses in older people, (especially degenerative conditions such as dementia, tumors, and chronic conditions), pain, and animals.

GEMS AND CRYSTALS: banded agate, desert rose, fossilized or petrified wood, fossils, leopardskin jasper, rutilated quartz, all the sand-colored and brown mottled jaspers, smoky quartz, tiger's eye, and zircon.

Gray

HEALING: lesions, wounds, burns, scalds, tissue and nerve connections, obsessions and acute anxiety, persistent pain, and illnesses for which a cause cannot be found or for which there is no effective treatment.

GEMS AND CRYSTALS: Apache tear (transparent obsidian), banded agate, labradorite, lodestone, meteorite, silvery hematite, and smoky quartz.

Black

HEALING: pain relief, constipation, irritable bowel syndrome, shields from side effects of invasive treatments (such as X-rays or chemotherapy), grief, and depression.

GEMS AND CRYSTALS: black coral, black opal, black pearl, jet, obsidian, onyx, snowflake obsidian, tektite, and tourmaline (schorl).

AN ALL-PURPOSE SELF-HEALING CRYSTAL METHOD

This is an excellent way of linking crystals with your own self-healing system and those of loved ones you heal, if you have not worked with crystal healing or healing before.

Choose what seems like the most suitable crystal color-wise from your crystals for the healing needed.

Alternatively, allow your hand to guide you over your crystal collection to select the right crystal. This could be different from one you would choose logically, as there can be hidden factors. For example, if you have a migraine, which would normally benefit from a purple crystal, a yellow one selected without looking could indicate that the source of the headaches could be a food allergy.

The Healing

Hold the chosen crystal in your open cupped hands and name the stone as representing whatever it is you want to lose, such as pain, fear, and symptoms of a chronic condition or a migraine.

As you hold the stone, imagine the stone getting heavier as it is filled with the pain, fear, or sickness. You may physically feel the stone getting heavier and your negative feelings or pain slowly ebbing away.

When the stone feels too heavy to hold or you sense it is full, wash it under running water, or if it is delicate, pass a floral incense stick over it counterclockwise and place it where light will shine on it.

You may need to do this many times if a condition is ongoing. Always use the same crystal.

CRYSTAL HEALING USING A SINGLE CRYSTAL

With crystal healing, all you need to do is to trust the chosen crystal to guide your hand through the right pathways through the body. Healing works through light clothing; and if you're healing someone else, that person may like a soft blanket for a covering.

Crystal healing is slow and you can light candles, burn fragrant oils, and play music to make it a pleasurable experience. Work with the minimum of dialogue so the patient relaxes—you can talk afterward, as you may have released a lot of worry. Relax, sit or stand, and allow the crystal to find its own movements, as you hold it two or three centimeters away from your body or that of a friend or family member. Generally the hand with which you write feels most natural, but trust yourself.

Begin a few centimeters above the right foot and move the crystal up the front of your body via your right leg and thigh. Pass your crystal slowly crisscrossing up the body via the left fingertips and arm, letting the crystal guide your hand as to its spiraling path. Go up to your face and hair and the top of your head and down via the right hand and arm and eventually out of the left foot. Your hand will spontaneously move the crystal counterclockwise to remove pain, tension, and unhappiness and clockwise to add light, warmth, energy, and hope. This holds true whether the problem is physical, emotional, spiritual, or as most usually are, a mixture of all three.

If the crystal spirals over a particular spot, the crystal has detected an energy knot. Allow the crystal to untangle this knot of trapped energy as you would a physical tangle of thread. Your crystal may also pause over a place on the body, and you will feel in your fingers as if it has momentarily run out of energy. This indicates a lifeless area where the energy has drained away or is blocked with tension. Lifeless areas will be automatically infused with smooth clockwise circular movements until you can feel the energy buzzing harmoniously again. Tune in and let the crystal do the work. When the crystal leaves your left foot, you will know healing is complete.

If you are healing other people, they can lie down. After you have healed the front of them, ask them to turn over so you can heal their back. Pass the crystal to heal the back of the body, this time from the top of the back of the head down the spine, again crisscrossing over both arms, right and left, down via the legs, left and right, and finally to the feet, left and right. Kneel or sit so you also are totally relaxed as you work.

Crystal healing is like a gentle swaying dance movement. If you are healing yourself, heal the back of your body by moving the crystal down to the nape of your neck after your head so you actually touch each shoulder at the back in turn, left and right, with the crystal; let it pause and the energy will flow down your back. When the back of your body feels in harmony, return the crystal to the front right shoulder and continue spiraling down to the right arm with the crystal a few centimeters away from the body again and continue as before. If you're healing yourself, your crystal may also pause several times on the front of the body and you will feel the energy passing through to the back of the body.

CRYSTAL PAIRS

Once you are confident with the single crystal method, you can heal with a pair of crystals to rebalance the energies in the body. This is a method to use to heal another person. Alternatively, you can do it alone exactly as you did with a single crystal by working through the front of the body via your shoulders (one crystal held in the opposite hand on each shoulder).

Initially choose a clear quartz or citrine in the hand you write with and a rose quartz or amethyst in the other.

For gentler healing, use a pair of amethysts.

If there are urgent health issues or ones in which conventional treatments are not working, use strong, vibrant opaque crystals such as red jasper or tiger's eye.

For pain, use two smoky quartz.

You can use crystal pairs with animals—soft muted colors or any of the brown earth agates.

Healing with Your Crystal Pairs

Practice moving both stones at the same time, the first or power stone in the hand with which you write circling clockwise and the second receptive stone moving in a counterclockwise direction.

Ask the person to lie back down on a bed, with closed eyes. Beginning a few centimeters above the right foot of the person you are healing and progressing up to the head, move the crystal pair on a parallel course so that they spiral and the whole body and cross over each other, again a few centimeters away from the body. The crystals will find their own pathways, so keep your hands loose and relaxed as you hold them. The stones will automatically increase movement in the areas of inner power points in the body and internal organs. The dual action is in itself healing and empowering, balancing the energies as they move. Sometimes the one stone will seem to be more active as the energies balance out.

If you encounter resistance, which you may sense as jaggedness or alternatively a blockage from the patient that you may feel in your own body, it indicates energy-flow stagnation or psychic knots. Allow the crystals to move in their own way to resolve the problem and then continue on their path. Repeat on the back of the body (ask the patient to roll over), starting at the top of the head and moving down the spine. Wherever you begin the healing you will spontaneously end on the back of the opposite foot from the one you began, to complete your circuit. Healing and balancing are complete.

After healing, stand with your feet apart and hands and fingers pointing down to allow any excess energy to flow out of your body. This is because the person you are healing will be perfectly balanced, but you will have absorbed excess energies from the patient and cosmos. However, some practitioners do, at the end of a healing before clearing themselves, pass their hands on either side of the patient's body, crown to feet and then below the feet so the hands meet about an extended armpsan to the patient's body to clear the auric or energy space. This is optional and easiest when a patient is lying down. Wash the crystals or smudge them by spiraling any floral incense stick over them.

ABSENT HEALING

For absent healing, use a small clear crystal sphere or any crystal egg, especially in blue, pink, purple, or green. The sphere can have marks or inclusions inside that will sparkle in the sun, moon, or candlelight. If you cannot get either of these, use any round smooth tumbled calcite or fluorite as a focus or an unpolished chunk of amethyst or rose quartz.

Light a pink or lilac candle, scented with rose or lavender if possible, so the light shines into the crystal. You can also work in sun- or moonlight but should still light a candle. Face the direction in which the person or animal lives or will be at the time of healing, visualizing him or her in a particular place in a room or garden. For a person or animal you have not met, use a photograph set in front of the candle. Holding the crystal in both hands, picture dark rays coming from the patient, entering the crystal, being transformed into circles of crystalline light, and floating like bubbles into the candle where they are taken back as light. Now place the crystal on the table and hold your hands over it, fingers pointing downward, not quite touching the crystal, until you can feel your fingers tingling. Picture streams of the white or colored crystalline light entering your fingers, flowing up though your heart, circulating around your body and down through your fingers again. When the power is buzzing in your fingers, with palms vertical, gently push the visualized light toward the direction of the person until your arms are fully outstretched with your palms still vertical.

Continue to return to the crystal, absorb more light, and gently push it into the cosmos, until you feel the power of the crystal slowing down and your own energies ebbing. Healing is now complete.

HEALING ANIMALS

If you are healing pets, use darker earthy crystals or soft muted ones in greens and browns, such as jade, moss or tree agate, banded agate, brown jasper, smoky or rutilated quartz, or fossilized wood. Young animals benefit from rose quartz or a pink calcite. An animal may allow you to stroke its fur, gently counterclockwise and then clockwise with a single crystal. Regardless of where the problem is, work first on the legs, the back, and the top of the head, avoiding tender places. Healing will flow through the animal to where it is needed most. Alternatively, when the animal or bird is asleep, face it about a foot and a half away and trace the outline of the animal in the air with the crystal as though your pet was standing or lying directly in front of you. Pass the crystal over the invisible form, feeling in your mind the soft fur or feathers until you feel a soft warm glow in your fingers.

FIVE CRYSTALS TO ADD TO YOUR COLLECTION

These are five of my favorite healing crystals for you to use and, if you wish, add to your growing collection of crystals.

1. Aragonite

Golden-brown aragonite, which can also be clear or orange, clears redundant anger lingering from old wrongs; slows the tendency to rush in and out of the home; brings reasoned opinions to workplace discussions in which personalities and scoring points dominate; shields people living alone and anyone in a place where there is anti-social behavior; and drives away bad dreams, as well as psychological or psychic attack, while sleeping.

As a crystal of the day, aragonite promises more harmonious ways of living and working but says you should avoid promising to do too much.

2. Chrysocolla

This bluish-green rich stone, often called the woman's wisdom stone, protects against domestic violence against and by both sexes, obstructive neighbors, and malice via social websites. It is a stone for older women to overcome prejudice against ageism and value natural beauty. Chrysocolla prevents a love partner straying or a business partner acting irresponsibly; it is also good for female businesses.

As a crystal of the day, chrysocolla says that experience will win over youthful enthusiasm; do not be steamrolled, for you do know best.

3. Howlite

White howlite with gray-or-black webbed veins is the crystal of physical health and strength and a desire for the highest standards of perfection. Howlite assists disabled adults or children in achieving potential, it is good for completing assignments on time without panicking, and it is a home-blessing stone when set over the front and back doors.

As a crystal of the day, white howlite says do not expect the impossible of yourself, as you have far higher standards than you expect of others.

4. Petrified or Fossilized Wood

This brown or fawn banded stone comes from fossilized trees in which the wood is replaced over many millions of years by a mineral. It can indicate the return of an old love, gives incentive for a new career or study after retirement or redundancy and is good for positive relationships with older family members and colleagues.

As a crystal of the day, fossilized wood says it is time to let go of a friendship or activity that no longer brings pleasure.

5. Selenite/Satin Spar

Orange, blue, and white glassy selenite with pearl-like luster is very similar to its sister satin spar that has bands of moving white light. Selenite reduces fears of rejection and is good for adults and children who fear the dark. Selenite jewelry is a natural luck, travel, love, and fertility charm and is excellent for older mothers or women who need medical intervention to conceive a child.

As a crystal of the day, selenite says you need to make the first move toward reconciliation with lovers or family members, especially mothers and children who have behaved unreasonably.

PERSONAL CRYSTALS

N O MATTER HOW MANY OR FEW CRYSTALS YOU have for daily use and healing, you will over the next few months, or even sooner, see a larger crystal that seems to choose you. You might find it in a market stall or for free on the seashore or you could ask for it as a birthday or holiday present if you have fallen in love with a particularly exquisite stone. The moment you touch it, the connection is made. But take your time and let it find you.

When you are tired, holding your special crystal will restore your energies; and if you're restless, it brings calm. Keep it in the center of your home to ensure abundance, health, and joy flow in and negativity or misfortune flow away. The longer you keep it, the more its energies grow.

To cleanse and empower, set it in a sheltered place in the open air on the night of the full moon; if you need extra energy for a particular date or venture, set the crystal from dawn or whenever you wake the day before till noon so the light shines on it.

For an infusion of luck, leave your special crystal outdoors on a starry night. The ideal date to fill it with natural energies is on Midsummer Day, around June 21 in the northern hemisphere and December 21 in the southern hemisphere.

ZODIAC CRYSTALS AND ANGELS

There are a number of different gems and crystals associated in various traditions for birth months with the zodiac signs under which we are born. I will give a more comprehensive list than usual, as I have suggested you also buy your zodiac crystal angel. If none of the birth crystals feels right, substitute a crystal in the color associated with your birth sign.

I will describe your crystalline zodiac angel and the special strengths that can be absorbed either from the angel or the associated crystal. Small crystal angels are relatively cheap and are a very potent source of energy and protection. Some crystals are ruled by more than one zodiac sign.

Buy a small angel for each member of the family—present, absent, and departed loved ones—adding one for each new birth or new older family member in the future. These you can keep in a circle in your crystal place. Add also any angels whose crystalline zodiacal strengths you need, even though they are not your own sign—for example, a moonstone angel for Muriel, zodiac angel of Cancer, to bring quiet sleep. Wear or carry your zodiac stone in a bag of the zodiac color at any time you need strength, protection, extra luck, or healing or want to be noticed in a positive way.

Zodiac crystals and angels are ideal as presents for a new baby, family member, or good friend on a milestone birthday, or for your partner on your wedding or moving in together. Give a single crystal once a year for a child—for example, as I suggested earlier in the book, a pearl or any crystal that can be made into a necklace to be given at eighteen, to be worn by the young adult or given to his or her future partner to make the link with their childhood years.

When it is a birthday or a special occasion or you need to send strength or healing to friends or family memebers, light their special zodiac candle color and hold their zodiacal crystal or angel to the light, sending blessings. Leave the candle to burn through. Of course, you can do this for yourself, too.

Aries, the Ram: March 21–April 20

GEMS AND CRYSTALS: blood agate, orange carnelian, polished gold chalcopyrite, diamond, silver iron pyrites, red jasper, rainbow, gold or silver sheen obsidian, pink rhodonite, red tiger's eye.

PLANET: Mars.

ELEMENT: fire.

RULING ANGEL: Machidiel (or Malahidael), warrior angel with sparkling golden-red halo and wings.

ANGELIC CRYSTALLINE STRENGTHS: self-confidence, strong identity, innovation, assertiveness, action, courage.

COLOR: red.

Taurus, the Bull: April 21–May 21

GEMS AND CRYSTALS: pink Andean opal, green chrysoprase, pink mangano calcite, emerald, jade, rainbow moonstone, rhodochrosite, rose quartz, pink tourmaline.

PLANET: Venus.

ELEMENT: earth.

RULING ANGEL: Asmodel or Ashmodel, angel of beauty surrounded by pink rays, creating what is of worth.

ANGELIC CRYSTALLINE STRENGTHS: persistence, patience, reliability, loyalty, practical abilities, stability, lovers of beauty.

COLOR: pink.

Gemini, the Heavenly Twins: May 22–June 21

GEMS AND CRYSTALS: agate, alexandrite, yellow calcite, lemon chrysoprase, citrine, yellow jasper, labradorite, opal, lemon quartz.

PLANET: Mercury.

ELEMENT: air.

RULING ANGEL: Ambriel or Ambiel, the messenger and travel angel wearing colors of early morning sunlight.

ANGELIC CRYSTALLINE STRENGTHS: excellent communication skills, adaptability, scientific/technological aptitude, curiosity, intelligence, versatility.

COLOR: pale yellow/gray.

Cancer, the Crab: June 22–July 22

GEMS AND CRYSTALS: white coral, moonstone, opalite, pearl, satin spar, selenite, cloudy or milky white quartz, clear topaz.

PLANET: Moon.

ELEMENT: water.

RULING ANGEL: Muriel, the silvery and pearl-robed healer angel with her magic carpet of dreams.

ANGELIC CRYSTALLINE STRENGTHS: sensitivity, kindness, imagination, homemaker, nurturer (especially of children), emotional security, ability to keep secrets, quiet sleep.

COLOR: silver.

Leo, the Lion: July 23–August 23

GEMS AND CRYSTALS: amber, fire opal, fire quartz, rainbow quartz, red spinel, ruby, white sapphire, sardonyx, sunstone.

PLANET: Sun.

ELEMENT: fire.

RULING ANGEL: Verchiel, the golden joy bringer who is surrounded by sunbeams.

STRENGTHS: power, courage, generosity, nobility, idealism, leadership, protection of the weak, ability to perform creatively in public.

COLOR: gold.

Virgo, the Maiden: August 24–September 22

GEMS AND CRYSTALS: amazonite, green calcite, green garnet, jade, white howlite, moss or tree agate, olivine, peridot, serpentine, snow quartz.

PLANET: Mercury.

ELEMENT: earth.

RULING ANGEL: Hamaliel or Hamaiel, angel of perfection, surrounded by misty forest green.

STRENGTHS: striving for perfection, organizational skills, methodical, attention to detail, efficiency, healing powers, ability to persevere a routine but necessary task though to the end, reliability.

COLOR: green.

Libra, the Scales: September 23–October 23

GEMS AND CRYSTALS: blue lace agate, blue chalcedony, chrysocolla, lapis lazuli, white or rainbow opal, blue quartz, rubellite/red tourmaline, blue sapphire.

PLANET: Venus.

ELEMENT: air.

RULING ANGEL: Zuriel, the teacher, the pale blue angel who brings calm and reason to any situation.

STRENGTHS: harmony, ability to see both sides of a situation, diplomacy, peacemaking skills, a strong sense of justice and charisma.

COLOR: light blue.

Scorpio, the Scorpion: October 24–November 22

GEMS AND CRYSTALS: black and red coral, hematite, mahogany obsidian, malachite, black obsidian, black opal, black pearl, red spinel, titanium aura, unakite.

PLANET: Pluto.

ELEMENT: water.

RULING ANGEL: Bariel, the angel of small miracles, who wears the colors of sunset.

STRENGTHS: intensity; religious, spiritual, and psychic awareness; ability to transform self and situations; the power to start over again or revive a stagnant situation.

COLOR: indigo, burgundy.

Sagittarius, the Archer: November 23–December 21

GEMS AND CRYSTALS: orange aragonite, aqua aura, azurite, iridescent bornite or peacock ore, chrysocolla, blue goldstone, goldstone, blue howlite, clear quartz, golden topaz, turquoise.

PLANET: Jupiter.

ELEMENT: fire.

RULING ANGEL: Adnachiel or Advachiel, the angel of learning and exploration with bright yellow robes.

STRENGTHS: expansiveness, love of travel and exploration, clear vision, seeker of truth, wide perspectives, flexibility, open-minded-ness, optimism, enthusiasm, creativity, especially in writing.

COLOR: bright yellow.

Capricorn, the Goat: December 22–January 20

GEMS AND CRYSTALS: green aventurine, bronzite, fossilized or petrified wood, red garnet, onyx, rubellite/red tourmaline, smoky quartz, tiger's eye, tourmalated quartz, black tourmaline.

PLANET: Saturn.

ELEMENT: earth.

RULING ANGEL: Anael or Hanael, the protector and archangel of love and fidelity, surrounded by green, silver, and roses.

STRENGTHS: wise caution, persistence regardless of opposition, respecter of tradition, ambition, self-discipline, loyalty, fidelity, and prudence with financial affairs.

COLOR: indigo, brown.

Aquarius, the Water Carrier: January 21–February 18

GEMS AND CRYSTALS: amethyst, Andean blue opal, angelite, blue celestite, blue quartz, sodalite, sugilite, titanium aura.

PLANET: Uranus.

ELEMENT: air.

RULING ANGEL: Cambiel, tall shadowy watcher or guardian archangel, guards you day and night from your own mistakes as well as external dangers.

STRENGTHS: idealism, independence, humanitarianism, inventiveness, detachment from swings of emotion or prejudices, unique perspective on the world.

COLOR: dark blue, purple.

Pisces, the Fish: February 19-March 20

GEMS AND CRYSTALS: aquamarine, clear aragonite, golden beryl, bloodstone, girosal quartz, pink and lilac kunzite, mother of pearl, ocean or orbicular jasper, watermelon tourmaline.

PLANET: Neptune.

ELEMENT: water.

RULING ANGEL: Barakiel or Barchiel, the blue and gold archangel of lightning and good luck, who has lightning flashing from his halo.

STRENGTHS: evolved intuitive powers, sympathy and empathy with others, weaver of myths, awareness of hidden factors, ability to merge with surroundings, alternative spirituality.

COLOR: soft white, mauve.

ANNIVERSARY GEMSTONES

Though there are traditional associations of particular gems and crystals with wedding anniversaries, you can give the zodiacal stone of the period in which the wedding fell or a crystal that has particular significance for you both.

OFFICIAL LIST OF THE
AMERICAN GEM TRADE ASSOCIATION˙

1ST ANNIVERSARY	GOLD JEWELRY
2ND ANNIVERSARY	GARNET
3RD ANNIVERSARY	CULTURED OR NATURAL PEARLS
4TH ANNIVERSARY	BLUE TOPAZ
5TH ANNIVERSARY	SAPPHIRE
6TH ANNIVERSARY	AMETHYST
7TH ANNIVERSARY	ONYX
8TH ANNIVERSARY	TOURMALINE
9TH ANNIVERSARY	LAPIS LAZULI
10TH ANNIVERSARY	DIAMOND JEWELRY
11TH ANNIVERSARY	TURQUOISE
12TH ANNIVERSARY	JADE
13TH ANNIVERSARY	CITRINE
14TH ANNIVERSARY	OPAL
15TH ANNIVERSARY	RUBY
16TH ANNIVERSARY	PERIDOT
17TH ANNIVERSARY	WATCHES
18TH ANNIVERSARY	CAT'S EYE
19TH ANNIVERSARY	AQUAMARINE
20TH ANNIVERSARY	EMERALD
21ST ANNIVERSARY	IOLITE

22ND ANNIVERSARY	SPINEL
23RD ANNIVERSARY	IMPERIAL TOPAZ
24TH ANNIVERSARY	TANZANITE
25TH ANNIVERSARY	SILVER
30TH ANNIVERSARY	CULTURED OR NATURAL PEARL
35TH ANNIVERSARY	EMERALD
40TH ANNIVERSARY	RUBY
45TH ANNIVERSARY	SAPPHIRE
50TH ANNIVERSARY	GOLD
55TH ANNIVERSARY	ALEXANDRITE
60TH ANNIVERSARY	DIAMOND

*Reproduced from *The New Crystal Bible* by Cassandra Eason, published by Carlton Books (UK) in 2010, and *The Complete Crystal Handbook*, published by Sterling US in 2010.

Cleansing and Empowering Your Personal Crystals

I have already suggested ways you can cleanse and empower your crystals after they have been used (see pages 9 and 11). However, for your special crystals, these are very gentle methods. Use this also for cleansing and empowering any delicate crystals.

If a crystal is pointed or angular, gently stroke it base to tip and down again to the base and up again to create a rhythmic movement.

For a round or oval crystal, hold it in the hand you do not write with, and with the index figure of the other hand, make spirals on the crystal surface until you connect with its innate rhythm or inner pulse, like a gentle throbbing.

Empower each crystal by blowing softly three times on it and between each breath, saying *Be* (breath) *for* (breath) *me* (or name the person, animal, or family for whom you are empowering the crystal). Then take another breath and name the purpose of the empowerment.

INDEX

Note: Page numbers in **bold** indicate primary references to crystals.